President and Congress DISCARD

Assessing Reagan's First Year

Edited by Norman J. Ornstein

American Enterprise Institute for Public Policy Research
Washington and London

Library of Congress Cataloging in Publication Data

Main entry under title:

President and Congress.

   (AEI symposia ; 82B)
   Contents: How the budget was won and lost/Allen
Schick—Congressional liaison in the Reagan White
House/Stephen J. Wayne—Reagan, Congress, and foreign
policy in 1981/I.M. Destler—[etc.]
   1. United States—Politics and government—1981
—Congresses. 2. Reagan, Ronald—Congresses.
I. Ornstein, Norman J. II. American Enterprise Institute
for Public Policy Research. III. Series.
E876.P73   973.927   82-6845

ISBN 0-8447-2237-5   AACR2

AEI symposia 82B

Printed in the United States of America

Contents

Contributors

I. M. DESTLER is senior associate at the Carnegie Endowment for International Peace, where he directs a project on executive-congressional relations in foreign policy. He has written *Making Foreign Economic Policy* and *Presidents, Bureaucrats and Foreign Policy*.

NORMAN J. ORNSTEIN is professor of politics at Catholic University, visiting scholar at the American Enterprise Institute, and political editor of "The Lawmakers" series on public television. His books include *The New Congress; Vital Statistics on Congress, 1980;* and *Interest Groups, Lobbying and Policymaking*.

ALLEN SCHICK is professor in the school of public affairs at the University of Maryland, College Park, and adjunct scholar at the American Enterprise Institute. He is the editor of *Public Budgeting and Finance,* the author of *Congress and Money: Budgeting, Spending and Taxing,* and *Reconciliation and the Congressional Budget Process*.

STEPHEN J. WAYNE is professor of political science at The George Washington University. His books include *The Legislative Presidency* and *The Road to the White House*.

Introduction

Norman J. Ornstein

No matter what their policy views, few people would challenge the assertion that 1981 was a remarkable year for American politics, particularly in the relations between president and Congress. By the end of the Carter administration, generalizations had multiplied about the inability of *any* president to get things through Congress or to get our hidebound political system to act. Ronald Reagan forced us to erase (or at a minimum to rewrite) those generalizations. He dominated the agenda and the outcomes in Congress during much of the year, in a fashion comparable only to the first years of Franklin Roosevelt and of Lyndon Johnson.

Given the striking features of 1981, the American Enterprise Institute's Congress Project convened a conference, as 1982 began, to assess presidential-congressional relations in Reagan's first year and to project the likely problems and prospects for the second year. The conference organizers were Thomas E. Mann and Norman J. Ornstein. Panels were held on economic policy, presidential-congressional liaison, foreign policy, and the overall process. In addition, Anthony King of the University of Essex, editor of AEI's forthcoming book on the president and Congress, *Both Ends of the Avenue,* offered a perspective from across the Atlantic.

All the conference participants gave President Reagan high marks for his first-year political performance. Assessments of the substance of his proposals and programs varied widely, however, as the remarks below suggest. Another consensus emerged on the prospects for 1982: Reagan faced tough sledding in the second session of the Ninety-seventh Congress.

Economic Policy

Allen Schick's paper assessed the numerous reasons for Reagan's stunning success on the budget and tax votes. Schick identified the Republi-

1

can majority in the Senate as a key factor in Republican unity. Commentary was provided by Stuart Eizenstat, formerly domestic adviser to President Jimmy Carter and now a Washington lawyer, and by Rudolph Penner, an AEI resident fellow, who was chief economist at the Office of Management and Budget during the Nixon and Ford administrations.

Eizenstat attributed much of the administration's success in 1981 to its novel use of the reconciliation process with the initial budget resolution—a tactic he attacked as "against the spirit of the Budget Act." Reconciliation, he said, was intended to be a limited action applied much later in the process, after the second budget resolution. By reversing its role, Congress turned its votes into "a parliamentary process by which, in effect, a president, like a prime minister, puts his entire package to an up-and-down vote without any limitations." He predicted that Congress would carefully scrutinize this process, which usurped the authority of both the appropriating and the authorizing committees.

Eizenstat also addressed himself to the question of economic predictions and assumptions. He said that the Reagan program may fall of its own weight because it is not realistic about future economic conditions. "The economy drives the budget to a much greater degree than the budget drives the economy," he emphasized. Drawing on his own experiences, he noted the pitfalls of faulty estimations; in a Carter budget, an underestimation of Treasury bill interest rates by a mere 2 percent meant that "we lost $13 billion to the deficit because our borrowing costs were higher than we had forecast." This can happen, he noted, with estimates made in good faith. It is impossible to come up with precise projections eighteen months before a budget takes effect. To Eizenstat, the Reagan budget for fiscal 1982 was surrounded by overoptimistic projections of strong economic growth, low unemployment, and high revenues.

The result is that high deficits are now projected. Without a strong economic performance, said Eizenstat, we can expect cracks in the Reagan budget-cutting coalition, with defections especially by moderate Republicans from the Northeast and the Midwest. "Those 'gypsy moth' Republicans will begin to look more toward their own elections."

Eizenstat gave credit to President Reagan's personal skills of persuasion in achieving his budget victories, adding, "There is no reason to think that they will diminish." He concluded, however, that the sluggish economy and the 1982 elections would make 1982 very different from 1981.

Rudolph Penner, even more pessimistic than Eizenstat about Reagan's second year, expressed concern over the way the budget process was applied in the first year and seemed likely to be distorted in the future. He anticipated severe difficulties stemming from the budget decisions of 1981, which "impose extraordinary pressures on politicians and political institutions and create grave risks for the economy." Although economically "a lot of good has been accomplished for the long run," politicians "live and die in the short run, and that looks bleak."

Referring to the second, *pro forma* budget resolution of 1981, Penner said:

> The plain fact is that there was no way Congress could politically tolerate an honest vote on a meaningful, realistic resolution last year. I don't see how they can do it this year, either. So we may see a whole series of *pro forma* or totally irrelevant resolutions in the future.
>
> If they are irrelevant, it will probably be because the resolutions make the same sort of unrealistic economic assumptions and promulgate unspecified spending—the same techniques that so distorted decision making last year.

Looking at the economy, Penner noted the severe problems posed by high interest rates and high deficits:

> If interest rates continue their recent rise, the expected 1982 recovery could, indeed, be jeopardized and the number of bankruptcies could continue to rise. The good done by the tax changes—and it is massive good when looked at in isolation— will be overwhelmed if my dire scenario comes to be. That is not the scenario I would predict. It is one I think we will barely avoid, but it is a risk that should be causing politicians some sleepless nights.

What solutions are there? Penner argued that the "easiest and most straightforward approach" would be to rescind a large part of the future tax cuts. Another resolution, he noted, "is called inflation. It is devastating economically and not very appealing politically, but its bad effects are delayed and not perceived immediately. That is why we have so much of it."

Penner hoped that this temptation would be avoided, but noted that "the pressures to monetize this huge debt are going to be enormous." Thus, he believed, the battles between the Federal Reserve Board, Congress, and the administration "may be the most dramatic and by far the most important battles of 1982."

Congressional Liaison

In the second session, Stephen J. Wayne assessed President Reagan's congressional liaison team and his relations with Congress generally. He described the Reagan liaison operation and contrasted it with that of Jimmy Carter. To explain Reagan's successes, he pointed to the ability of the administration to limit and control the congressional calendar and to the liaison team's effective performance through the transition and into the first year. He emphasized, however, that controlling the agenda would be a much greater problem for Reagan in 1982.

The first commentator, William Gribbin, deputy assistant to the president for legislative affairs, attributed much of the success of the administration's legislative program to the philosophical coherence of Reagan's proposals. As a former Senate Republican staffer, Gribbin recalled that President Carter's initiatives "fell of their own weight because . . . the ideas on which they were based no longer cohered."

The Reagan administration had succeeded in Congress, Gribbin suggested, by and large because its proposals "related to decisions that, at their heart, are not political." Because the proposals were embodied in a conservative philosophical framework, "Congress could expect rather less waffling from us on all sorts of things." He said that many Nixon and Ford legislative proposals were fought over *political* battle lines with Democrats. Consequently, the lack of an ideological frame of reference caused their failure.

Gribbin cast doubt on Wayne's assumption that a key to Reagan's legislative victories lay in the "return to normalcy"—that the White House was ready to do some old-fashioned horse-trading and political arm-twisting. He indirectly criticized the notion that if you lean hard enough on congressmen, they will make a deal: "It is not true that we never make a deal, but I think we have altered that part of normalcy [by appealing to members with an ideologically coherent package] in a very healthy way."

Gribbin debunked the widely held view that the administration will stay away from social issues: "What makes anybody think that Ronald Reagan would want to sit on the sidelines of social issues? Let us not assume that the administration intends to rerun 1981 [stressing budget and tax policy] from year to year." In fact, Gribbin said of White House participation on social issues:

> If I were . . . of a mischievous bent, I would do what I could to have the House of Representatives vote on four or five controversial social issues, in each case knowing, as indeed we know, that there is a majority in that body solidly on the president's side—a majority that would include in each case about one-third of the Democrats, more Democrats than supported the administration on the economic package.

Bill Cable, formerly President Carter's chief of congressional liaison for the House of Representatives, agreed with Wayne's point about agenda control and praised the Reagan transition process. He addressed himself largely to the contrast between Carter and Reagan.

Cable said that because Carter was an activist president, he thought it necessary to push a smorgasbord of issues rather than one entree at a time. He and Carter believed that "there is a very high correlation between what is accomplished in the four years of an executive's term . . . and what is proposed in the first year, especially if the president is an activist who wants to do a lot of things." Cable also said that Reagan's agenda was sweeter to swallow than Carter's: a tax cut and the promise of prosperity sound better than energy conservation, sacrifice, and a change in the life style of thirty years.

Cable faulted Carter (and indirectly praised Reagan's opposite tack) for not exercising enough White House control over the liaison office appointments at cabinet departments and government agencies. He suggested that since many of Carter's agency lobbyists were from the Washington establishment they were captives of their constituencies and would not fight hard for the president's proposals.

Cable charged that the Reagan no-compromise approach on the budget could cause long-run tensions within Congress. The demand for precise budget cuts could cause tensions between the ranking minority member of a committee and its chairman, who are usually inclined to compromise: "This administration . . . has played a very high-risk game with the Congress. . . . They have proposed and then demanded 99 percent of what they asked for, or better." Cable saw severe problems ahead for the administration if it pursued this strategy in 1982.

Charles O. Jones, professor of political science at the University of Virginia, cautioned that political observers make a mistake when they try to define Reagan's legislative successes by standards set by, say, Johnson: "There is no one formula for success. Relations depend on political and policy circumstances that are different among presidents, different among Congresses, and different over time within an administration." The "universal" component of good White House–Capitol Hill relations is "mutual respect between the two sets."

Jones offered his own list of the reasons for Reagan's victories, giving Reagan and his staff high marks for knowing:

1. that the White House is the center of politics and that the president is the chief politician
2. how to set priorities
3. that Congress has a legitimate role to play in public policy
4. how to work the system (Republican Senate and Democratic House)
5. how to add and how to use the favors available to the president to make sure that one and one stay two
6. that electoral victory is only one source of power and cannot be used to hit people over the head

7. that Congress itself was interested in making some policy changes

Jones also gave the Reagan team credit for understanding the potential for presidential power in the reformed congressional budget process —a process that was intended by Congress to get back at an earlier president, Richard Nixon, but that is still "up for grabs" for Congress or the president to use to advantage.

Jones emphasized, however, that 1982, an election year, would be more of a challenge for the president. The question for the second year would be whether Reagan was able to adapt to the changing conditions.

A View from Britain

Anthony King of the University of Essex offered a transatlantic perspective on Reagan's first year with Congress, drawing comparisons with the longer experience of Margaret Thatcher in Britain and suggesting, on the basis of Thatcher's two years, that Reagan would face difficulties in the future. While one might expect a prime minister with a sizable party majority to rule with ease in a parliamentary system, Thatcher has had no easy time of it in Britain.

One root of her problem, King emphasized, is the increasing independence of back-bench members of Parliament. King made three major points about change in the British legislature:

1. "Nowadays all British members of Parliament are good constituency members." They go home to their districts, hold town meetings, and answer constituent mail.

2. The establishment of investigative (but not legislative) committees in the House of Commons has given MPs, even members of the government's party, opportunities to challenge government policies. "To a remarkable extent, on these committees, party lines tend to break down." By criticizing government policies, "back-bench members of Parliament [are] beginning to feel their strength."

3. "Party discipline in the British House of Commons is declining very substantially indeed." In 1955 defections from the party line occurred in only 2 percent of House of Commons votes. In 1974, however, "there were rebellions in 28 percent of the votes."

King added that the independence phenomenon has increased the power of back-bench MPs. They now realize that if they do not support the government, even on a major issue, and it loses on a vote in Parliament, the government will not necessarily fall. "This has had the effect of very substantially increasing the power and influence of back-bench members of Parliament. . . . They are actually getting their way."

What does this all mean? King predicted that "within the next eighteen months or the next two years, there is going to be massive pressure on the part of back-bench Tory MPs in the government to try to get the government to change course. . . . I think the Thatcher administration is going to be in extreme difficulty from its own side of the political fence, including from the many businessmen whose oxen are being gored by the same kinds of phenomena that you find in this country." The implications for Reagan's second year, said King, are obvious.

Foreign Policy

I. M. Destler, of the Carnegie Endowment for International Peace, assessed the foreign policy of Reagan's first year. He noted that, in the first half of 1981, even as the president was racking up stunning economic victories, the administration's record on foreign policy was "anything but impressive." In the second half of 1981, the administration became more pragmatic, more modest in its goals, more willing to compromise on foreign policy—and, as a result, more successful. Destler reviewed the various foreign policy issues of 1981, concentrating particularly on the sale of Airborne Warning and Control System (AWACS) planes to Saudi Arabia and on foreign aid. On the AWACS sale, he concluded, the president did not triumph, as he did on economic policy; he merely survived. On foreign aid, a pragmatic approach resulted in a victory, the first foreign aid bill in three years to pass Congress.

The first discussant, Douglas J. Bennet, assistant secretary of state for congressional relations in the Carter administration, said that the Reagan administration wisely avoided engaging in political trade-offs to secure congressional support for its foreign policy initiatives. "Logrolling" is of "limited value. . . . It is not sufficiently dignified." He endorsed Reagan's approach of making the case for a foreign policy initiative "on the strength of the issues themselves." Like Destler, Bennet stressed that building a "moderate bipartisan" consensus incrementally is the only way to secure congressional support for an administration's foreign policy. "The votes are not there" for radical departures in foreign policy. He added that Reagan's creative use of the presidential letter, which gave wavering senators a way to support the AWACS sale, was an important innovation in presidential lobbying techniques to gain congressional support for a proposal. "It has wonderful possibilities, and its use should be expanded."

Although Bennet endorsed the Reagan administration's tactics in gaining congressional approval for its foreign policy, he questioned its intellectual underpinnings; he described Reagan's initial foreign policy as some "perniciously ill informed" notions about how the rest of the world

7

works. He also said that the administration's absence of a clearly defined overall foreign policy hindered congressional approval of the AWACS sale, while the absence of a human rights policy contributed to the rejection of Ernest Lefever's nomination to be assistant secretary of state for human rights.

Bennet expressed his belief that the failure to establish a coherent American foreign policy is not limited to the current administration:

> I think that the machinery that we have for legitimizing foreign policy in the United States to the Congress is creaky. The quality of our leadership is inadequate, and this is not a question of Democrats or Republicans. It is the track record for many years.

Yet he did not see a structural solution. He noted that "there is no institutional mechanics or fiddling that will address this problem. Thoughtful and reasonable leadership in executive and legislative branches" is needed, he said, "to spend the time it takes . . . and take the political heat" to develop "adequate foreign policy" and "sell it to the American people." Congress, he stressed, will always be a part of the decision-making process in this area.

Alton Frye, Washington director of the Council on Foreign Relations, gave the following overall assessment:

> The question 1981 left us with is whether the pragmatism that showed up late in the year on a number of foreign policy issues reflects a true evolution that will shape the rest of the administration's foreign policy and its relations with Congress . . . or . . . was a deviation from a steady, continuous commitment to a one-dimensional foreign policy.

Frye observed that there seems to be "a struggle continuing for the soul of this administration" on foreign policy between the forces of "sophisticated internationalist anti-Sovietism" and the forces of narrow, go-it-alone unilateralism. Although there are some signs of encouragement for the growth of pragmatic internationalism, the overall record to date does not leave Frye confident about its future.

Frye also drew some lessons from the AWACS vote, comparing Reagan's success on it to Carter's success in gaining confirmation for Paul Warnke as arms control negotiator. In both cases the support and opposition split very sharply on partisan lines. The AWACS vote, like the Warnke nomination, "could be the harbinger of a partisan split . . . not to be encouraged by a president who needs bipartisan support." Frye did not think the AWACS victory would give Reagan momentum for further foreign policy successes in Congress; he expended too much political capital to turn it to his advantage in the future.

Finally, Frye urged caution in regard to Reagan's position on defense. Although there is widespread recognition of the need to enhance our defense capability, the massive defense commitments called for in future Reagan budgets would be hard to sustain or to justify in coming months.

Commentator Melvin Laird, former congressman and secretary of defense, noted the breadth of Destler's review of 1981, but emphasized one glaring omission: Reagan's most important foreign policy initiative in 1981 began at home—increasing defense spending. "The most important foreign policy issue in the mind of voters [in the 1980 election] was rebuilding the nation's defenses." Laird said that it is paramount "for any new administration to address the issues foremost in the minds of the voters" in its first year. He also said that a strengthened national defense is a very practical tool to implement foreign policy. An enhanced security posture is critical in assuring our allies that we will be able to live up to our treaty obligations, "the supreme law of this land."

Laird did not endorse every particular of the Reagan defense program; in some areas, he thought, "we went a little too far." But, he added, as far as readiness and personnel go:

> You have to give the Congress, the administration, and the Department of Defense very high marks. . . . The communication and exchange the administration had with the committees of the Congress in this area show how congressional-executive relationships can be carried out in an extraordinarily fine way.

Laird added that, in his view, the AWACS vote was not a major foreign policy issue. It was elevated to that status only when Defense and State Department officials failed "to carry out their responsibilities and keep enough senators and members of the House uncommitted on a veto issue." The issue "should never have got to the White House in the first place." Laird put the Lefever fiasco in the same category, blaming not Reagan but the State Department:

> I really think it is unfair for people, particularly in the academic area, always to point the finger at the White House if anything goes wrong. If you are going to have live, working departments, if you are going to give them responsibility, you should make them responsible for those confirmations, and they should be doing the background work.

Assessing Reagan's First Year

In the final session, Norman J. Ornstein of AEI and Catholic University offered praise for President Reagan's ability to define and dominate the national and congressional agenda in 1981; he contrasted Reagan's

9

performance and experience with those of President Carter. He stressed, however, that the last four months of 1981 were not like the first eight months: they were much tougher, and the president was frequently forced to compromise with Congress. He believed that 1982 would probably be like the last four months of 1981, a more typical year—tough going for the president in Congress, with a series of inconclusive guerrilla battles and little dramatic movement.

The first commentator, Representative Richard B. Cheney (Republican, Wyoming), former White House chief of staff to Gerald Ford, gave much credit for Reagan's success on Capitol Hill to members of Congress. He praised the Republican congressional leaders "who struggled in the House to deliver majority votes for the president" and some Democrats, including Budget Committee Chairman James Jones (Democrat, Oklahoma) and Majority Whip Thomas Foley (Democrat, Washington), for allowing an up-or-down vote on the Reagan program. Cheney noted that the budget victories came about in part because of "the willingness of many Democrats to support the integrity of the [budget] process." They could have scuttled it at various stages during the debate "for the sake of partisan advantage, and they didn't."

Cheney agreed with Ornstein in emphasizing Republican unity in Congress as the key to Reagan's budget victory. The degree of GOP unity was "phenomenal," while the number of Democratic defectors was "about the norm." "It is relatively easy for a 'boll weevil' to vote to support Ronald Reagan—he is voting his district." On the other hand, when it comes to "gypsy moth" Republicans, "It is much more difficult for them to vote to support the president's program, and that is a point that needs to be made."

Cheney also emphasized the contribution of both Reagan's persuasive skills and the administration's "creative" use of the 1974 Budget and Impoundment Control Act to the budget success. On the AWACS issue, however, he criticized the administration's performance and commented that the president may have expended too many resources and too much credit "to get four airplanes for the Saudis." When he needs that political capital later on as other key issues arise, "that decision may come back to haunt us."

Like Ornstein, Cheney saw a clash ahead between the "social" issues like busing and abortion and the continuing economic concerns:

> There are a great many of us who are eager to avoid the social issues and to push them on the back burner for 1983 or 1984; to have economic issues, budget, and tax questions crowd out those other concerns that frankly are divisive where our party is concerned and, in my mind, do not have a lot to do with the mandate that we received in the 1980 election.

Though Cheney, too, saw turbulent times ahead for Reagan, with much more confrontation in Congress, he did not see the president as powerless or unable to influence events or outcomes. "The president has an awful lot of tools available to help him achieve his objectives, and he has by no means shot every arrow in his quiver yet."

Eugene Eidenberg, director of the Democratic National Committee, suggested that the heavy press emphasis on the significance of Reagan's electoral victory in 1980 helped the president win legislative support for his economic program. But Eidenberg did not think that Republicans in Congress could build reelection campaigns on Reagan's legislative successes. "The electoral results in November 1982 and November 1984 will not be an expression of the additive effects of how many victories versus how many defeats he had on Capitol Hill." Rather, these elections will depend on the public's reaction to Reagan's economic recovery program, its basics now in place. A continued adverse reaction will be a hindrance to Republicans in 1982 and 1984. Republicans in Congress up for reelection and tied to the president's coattails "will be asked to be accountable for their records as they relate to the unemployment rate, to the recession, and to the mysterious effects of supply-side economics."

Eidenberg, a former assistant for intergovernmental relations under President Carter, also addressed the question of intergovernmental relations in light of President Reagan's economic policy. He asserted that the radical restructuring of federal, state, and local responsibilities that has resulted was less a function of philosophy than the "driving wedge of budget and tax decisions that have radically altered the revenue picture that faces all levels of government in this country."

As state and local governments face the resulting hard decisions about cutting services and increasing taxes, an interesting political question emerges: Who will be blamed—the administration or governors, state legislators, and their county and city council counterparts? Eidenberg stressed that Democrats "will spend some time and some money in 1982 trying to ensure that this political responsibility stays at 1600 Pennsylvania Avenue and with the members of Congress who voted for those budget and tax bills."

David Gergen, assistant to President Reagan for communications, stressed the personal leadership qualities of the president over the circumstances he inherited. "President Reagan deserves a good deal of credit for shaping the circumstances that existed when he came here."

Gergen challenged the underlying assumption he saw in Ornstein's paper "that presidents are interchangeable, that a Carter or a Nixon or a Ford, in similar circumstances, could have produced similar results." He contrasted, for example, Carter's and Reagan's skills in delivering a television address, adding, "I think all of us are still struggling to explain why Reagan was so successful versus some other presidents in their first year."

While Reagan stands in contrast to his predecessors, the White House staff did profit greatly from a review of the experiences of previous presidents during their first hundred days. Among the lessons learned, according to Gergen:

• The first few months of a presidency is "the time when a president really establishes an agenda." An administration could control that agenda by setting "a very limited number of goals" and focusing on those.

• The early days are the time when a president "establishes his public persona as president; up to that time he is seen either as a campaign figure or as a private person."

• The first one hundred days are the period when a president "can make his biggest mistakes, the mistakes that may mar him throughout his presidency."

Gergen said that the White House staff let Reagan's personality "take care of itself, worked hard on a single-minded agenda," and was careful to avoid serious early mistakes. He emphasized the importance of the changing public perception of Reagan after he was shot. This was a moment when we saw a public official as he truly is, and it formed a lasting impression: "Added to the affability was a quality of courage and grace that . . . has served him extremely well for the rest of the time he has been in office."

Looking to 1982, Gergen said that the White House was very much aware of the difficulties ahead. He conceded that the administration would find itself negotiating more with the Democratic leadership to win support for legislative proposals. But he also said that the White House would not shy away from using the reconciliation process to win the next budget battle: "I do believe that the vote on reconciliation allows you to express the philosophical views of the members of the House in a way up-and-down votes on some individual issues do not allow you to do as easily or as well." Gergen was also optimistic about the 1982 elections. Although he labeled the Republicans underdogs, he felt that Reagan's personal popularity and campaign skills would be assets in the campaign.

Gergen said that there were "hints" in the 1980 elections of a possible realignment in the American body politic, though it had not yet occurred. More important, Reagan had a core of support of perhaps 30 to 40 percent of the population. Neither President Ford nor President Carter had such a core. Reagan had even more of a reservoir: "beyond the core," said Gergen, "I think there is another healthy percentage of the population who want to give him more of a chance." Thus 1982 looked tough, but doable.

The final commentator, Nelson W. Polsby of the University of California, Berkeley, contrasted Washington opinion and public opinion in assessing a president. He called realignment theories a "Washington phenomenon" for which there is little empirical evidence: "But if you look at hard indicators of these kinds of things, it [realignment] is very difficult to spot." Issue polling, party identification numbers, and other sources of public opinion reveal no realigning shift to the Republicans. Polsby also said that Reagan's standing in public opinion polls is lower than that of any of his immediate predecessors after their first year in office.

Polsby noted that 1981 was not just Reagan's first year—it was Howard Baker's first year (as Senate majority leader) and Bob Michel's first year (as House Republican leader), and their first years were successes, too. To understand the whole picture, we need to know more about how, why, and under what conditions Baker and Michel were able to hold the "gypsy moths" in the Republican coalition—particularly to assess their "staying power." Polsby also pointed out that "the number of Southern Democrats who could be counted on to vote with the Republicans has, in fact, shrunk dramatically." The concentration on Reagan's legislative victories has "overshadowed" the longer-term issue of how long the coalitions of "gypsy moths" and "boll weevils" will remain intact and how the coming elections will influence their composition.

How the Budget Was Won and Lost

Allen Schick

In 1981, Ronald Reagan won the battles but lost the budget. On four issues he challenged congressional Democrats and obtained the legislation he demanded. The first budget resolution was crafted according to his specifications, as was the reconciliation bill it triggered. The president also emerged victorious in a bidding war over tax legislation. His final triumph came in the closing days of the session when Congress approved a continuing appropriation that satisfied most of his demands.

Although it was the most visible battleground, Capitol Hill was not the only one, nor was it the one that mattered the most for the president's ambitious economic and budgetary objectives. The president was losing in the marketplace, as high interest rates, rising unemployment, and a deepening recession shattered the promise of a balanced budget by 1984. According to some recent forecasts, deficits in excess of $100 billion a year are likely until mid-decade. Worse yet, the deficits will grow even if the economy improves. There is considerable apprehension that rising deficits during periods of economic growth will trigger a new spiral in interest rates and will abort the next recovery before unemployment has significantly abated.

One should, however, be wary of gloom and doom predictions on the basis of less than one year's performance. Gerald Ford went through a difficult first year (in a shortened administration), and the economy was substantially improved by the end of his term, though not enough to effect his reelection. Ronald Reagan might be right in arguing that his policies have only recently gone into effect and that it will take months or years to recover from underinvestment, low productivity, high inflation, excessive regulation, and overdependence on federal assistance. Still, one thing cannot be denied: the buoyant plans presented to Congress and to the American people in February and March 1981 will not be achieved. Instead of growing, the economy has declined; instead of shrinking, the deficit has grown; instead of leveling off, federal spending has continued to climb. The rise in fiscal 1982 expenditures might be as much as that of fiscal 1981.

14

The unraveling of the budget has been particularly damaging because Ronald Reagan staked the success of his administration on the performance of the budget and the economy. The president did not take the position that the economy goes through self-correcting business cycles and that, consequently, it would be better for the federal government to remain on the sidelines than to try to solve current economic ills. His ultimate aim might be less intervention, but in his first year the president was an active and determined intervener who spent much of his time and political resources on budgetary issues. In 1981, the president spoke more often to the American people on budget matters than on all other issues combined. He allowed the budget to crowd out other objectives that had emerged during his successful campaign, and, with the exception of the sale of AWACS planes to Saudi Arabia, the budget was the issue that defined his relationship with Congress.

Congress responded by behaving more as a budget office than as the legislative branch.[1] The Senate took almost 200 votes on budget issues in 1981, not including the roll calls on regular appropriations bills and the budget battles fought over authorizing legislation, such as food stamps and agriculture. More than two-thirds of the recorded votes in the Senate were on budget-related matters.

Because of the limitations under which it operates, the House of Representatives had far fewer budget-related votes, but its relationship with the White House was defined in a half-dozen key votes that pitted the Democratic majority against Ronald Reagan. The president prevailed on each of those votes, as he did time and again in the Senate.

How were the president's legislative triumphs transformed into budgetary and economic defeats? Millions of words have been filed by journalists and other observers in the media blitz on the budget. The depth of reporting and sustained attention have been extraordinary by American journalistic standards. Few articles have been as instructive as William Greider's profile of Budget Director David Stockman in the December 1981 issue of *Atlantic Monthly*. It should be read as the education of the American people, not only of Stockman. Stripped of its ad hominem fascination with an heroic budget master, that article could have been titled "How the Budget Was Won and Lost."

All the answers have been given; I cannot claim any special insight or interpretation. My purpose in this paper is to distill what happened in 1981 through one person's perspective and to provide a glimpse at what Reagan's first year as the nation's chief budget maker might portend for his next.

---

1. The distinction between "legislation" and financial matters dates to the nineteenth century and is still inscribed in the rules of the House and Senate.

Hegemony in the Senate

The public confrontations between the White House and House Democratic leaders and the president's success in attracting dissident Democrats to his cause garnered the lion's share of media attention. O'Neill versus Reagan was high drama; the wooing and winning of the "boll weevils" (conservative Southern Democrats) made an exciting story. But the key to presidential success was held in the Senate, not in the House, and by Republicans, not by Democrats. The president carried the day because of Republican cohesion, without which no likely number of Democratic defections would have sufficed. The Senate was critical for the president because it had long been the bastion of liberal spending attitudes. Continuing a trend that had begun in the 1970s, however, the Senate put a conservative stamp on the budget in 1981.

The first major budget vote occurred on February 6, two weeks before the president unveiled his budget plans to Congress. On that day, fifty Senate Republicans voted for an increase in the statutory limit on the public debt. Despite decades of Republican protests over chronic deficits and the national debt, not a single Republican dissented. There were, to be sure, simple explanations for this turnabout. The Republicans did not want to embarrass their new president by refusing to let the federal government finance its debts. Moreover, they regarded the debt increase as a legacy of past Democratic profligacy over which they had no control and for which they could not be held responsible. But this early test was not merely a closing of the books on the past; it was a clue to future Republican behavior. Senate Republicans were confident that this was one of the last debt increases that they would be called upon to support. They believed that the new administration would rein in federal spending, that the unrelenting trend of the past half-century would be halted. They had a friend in the White House, but much more important, they had the votes in their own ranks. For the first time in a generation, the Republicans were in charge of the Senate. Only two of these Republican senators had been members the last time that happened, almost thirty years earlier. Sixteen Republicans were newly elected; another eighteen were still in their first term.

It was a heady time for this mostly young band of Republicans. They felt they could make a difference, not only in the policies of government, but in the political composition of America as well. Theirs was the opportunity to shrink the size of the federal government and to reclaim majority status for the Republican party. They were determined not to repeat the me-tooism that had plagued their party in the past. They—and the president—had a mandate for change, and they acted on that basis.

They could succeed, however, only if they held together, and party unity was not easy to accomplish. For more than a generation the

Senate had grown comfortable with blurred party lines. Senators were wont to vote according to their convictions and interests, and party identification was weaker in the upper chamber than in the House. Moreover, despite the conservative tide in 1980, the Republicans still had quite a few moderates and liberals in their ranks. On the basis of past voting patterns, one would have expected Senate Republicans to go their separate ways, especially on budgetary issues.

In the Senate, budget resolutions were devoid of party labels. Beginning in 1975, Senators Edmund Muskie (Democrat, Maine) and Henry Bellmon (Republican, Oklahoma), at the time the chairman and ranking minority member of the Senate Budget Committee, had forged a bipartisan coalition that ensured broad support for budget resolutions. Muskie and Bellmon were convinced that the new budget process would be impotent if their committee and the Senate were divided along party lines. Through their cooperation, it became common for budget resolutions to pass by majorities of 2 to 1 or better.[2]

Bipartisanship in the Senate, however, meant schism in Republican ranks. The first time the Senate approved a budget resolution in 1975, nineteen Republicans voted for passage while eighteen were opposed. Thirteen budget resolutions were adopted by the Senate from 1975 through 1980; on each, at least one-third of the Republicans disagreed with the majority within their party. Over the six-year span, Republicans cast 229 votes against passage of the resolutions and 219 votes for passage.

Senate Republicans abandoned bipartisanship in 1981, preferring to make their deals with the White House rather than with Democratic colleagues.[3] This strategy succeeded because the president was able to unite the Republicans to an extent truly extraordinary in the annals of the Senate. The attitudes that knitted the Republicans together on the debt-ceiling bill persisted through dozens of key votes. Only one Senate Republican voted against the budget resolution approved in March 1981; only two opposed the resolution adopted in May. The Republicans were unanimous in their support of the reconciliation bill, while two broke ranks on the *pro forma* second resolution adopted near the close of the session.[4]

2. For an examination of congressional budget practices, see Allen Schick, *Congress and Money: Budgeting, Spending, and Taxing* (Washington, D.C.: Urban Institute, 1981).

3. In 1981, the Republicans voted together 81 percent of the time on "party unity" votes compared with 65 percent of the time in 1980. See *Congressional Quarterly Weekly Report*, January 9, 1982, pp. 61-65.

4. The second budget resolution retained the budget levels set forth in the first resolution, despite the fact that changing economic conditions made it highly unlikely that the original targets would be met. For this reason, it is regarded as a *pro forma* resolution rather than a genuine set of budget decisions.

Even more telling than these votes on passage was Republican cohesion on floor amendments. Throughout the year, Senate Democrats offered a blizzard of amendments, some to harass the opposition, some as genuine alternatives. With only a six-seat margin in the Senate, the Republicans might have lost if only a handful defected. This rarely happened, however, as the Republicans repeatedly united against Democratic attacks. The Democrats offered twenty-eight amendments to a "preliminary" budget resolution;[5] only one attracted more than eight Republican votes, and that was on a proposal to deepen the spending cuts proposed by the Budget Committee. Six times, the Republicans voted en bloc against the Democrats; five times, all but one Republican voted with the party; on seven of the votes, there were only two defections. The Republicans stood together on the first budget resolution and on the reconciliation bill. On a series of Democratic amendments to retarget the tax reductions, the Republicans averaged fewer than two defections. Even when the Democratic amendments were "popular," they failed to crack Republican unity. Only three Republicans sided with the opposition on lowering the tax rates for two-income households; only six voted to increase tax assistance for the elderly.

Perhaps the most remarkable display of Republican unity came at the end of the session when the Democrats coalesced behind a string of amendments to the defense appropriation bill. As we shall see later, appropriations votes usually do not follow party lines. Nevertheless, the Republicans offered a unified response to the Democratic strategy, with unanimous opposition to eight of the amendments and an average of two defections overall.

Although this mood change was the key factor in Republican cohesion, the leadership skills of Majority Leader Howard Baker contributed significantly to welding rank-and-file Republicans into a loyal and effective majority. When the Republicans unexpectedly captured the Senate and propelled him into the leadership position, Baker quickly decided to mobilize the Senate into an instrument of presidential power. Rather than establish an independent power center, Baker decided to cast his lot with the White House, helping to push the president's program through the Senate but also informing the president of the things that mattered to his colleagues. One of Baker's first decisions, taken in cooperation with Senator Pete Domenici (Republican, New Mexico), the new chairman of the Budget Committee, was to put the president's budget on a "fast track" by bringing a budget resolution to the floor before the period set in the budget act. The resolution approved by the

5. The Budget Act provides for adoption of the first resolution by May 15, but the Senate considered a "preliminary" resolution before the Easter recess as a means of pressuring the House to act on the president's program.

Senate in March never made it to the House, but it gave clear notice that the president would get what he wanted from the Senate.

Baker was aided in his effort to unify the Republicans by the fact that most of them shared the president's economic and budgetary objectives. Over the previous decade, the number of liberal and moderate Republicans in the Senate had dwindled, and the remainder did not want to challenge the president openly at the start of his administration. Moreover, on many issues Baker could count on conservative Democrats to offset any defections in his own ranks. During debate on the preliminary resolution, for example, moderate Republican John Chafee (Rhode Island) offered an amendment to restore about $1 billion of the spending reductions. Although eleven Republicans voted for the restoration, a larger number of Democrats sided with the president, and the amendment was defeated. The vote on Chafee's amendment was one of the few instances in which a large number of Republicans broke with the president.

The price of Republican unity was polarization of the Senate. If the Republicans were more cohesive, so, too, were the Democrats.[6] Once budgetary bipartisanship crumbled, the Democrats felt compelled to devise party alternatives to the president's program. The president thus succeeded not only in strengthening party identification among the Republicans, but in unifying the Democrats as well. As long as the president could prevail by confronting the Democrats, he did not have to subject his budget to the interparty bargaining that had once been commonplace in the Senate. But this strategy had two limitations, which shall be considered later in this chapter. First, where there is confrontation, there can be no consensus. In my view, some of the difficult political and economic issues facing the nation cannot be resolved by the divisive tactics that served the president so well in 1981. Second, party loyalty cannot be called into play on every budget issue. The highly aggregated decisions made in budget resolutions can be more easily cast as party votes than can the disaggregated votes on appropriations bills. Republicans—and Democrats—have been less cohesive on appropriations than on budget matters.

The House Divided

The president's situation in the House was far different from the one he faced in the Senate. In the House the president already had a unified party, but it lacked majority status. From 1975 through 1980, House Republicans were steadfast in their opposition to the budget resolutions

6. As calculated by the *Congressional Quarterly,* Democratic unity in the Senate increased from 64 percent to 71 percent.

formulated by the Democratic leadership. On average, 95 percent of the Republicans voted against adoption of the budget resolutions during these years; but because they were outvoted by the Democrats, all of the resolutions prescribed by the budget act won House approval.

An examination of the 1975–1980 voting pattern, however, should have convinced the Republicans that they had a good chance of prevailing in the House in 1981. For one thing, the Republicans had significantly risen from their post-Watergate nadir and had closed two-thirds of the gap between the number of Republicans and the number of Democrats in the House. Ronald Reagan had almost fifty more Republicans (and faced fifty fewer Democrats) in the House than Gerald Ford had in 1975. Furthermore, even with their big majorities, the Democrats had difficulty getting their budget resolutions through the House. Twice, the margin was only four votes; twice, the resolution was rejected and had to be revised to obtain House approval. Moreover, during the six years of congressional budgeting, the Democrats had suffered serious defections on every budget resolution. At least thirty-eight House Democrats deserted the leadership on each of the budget resolutions; over the six years, there was an average of sixty-four defections on the Democratic side. The Democrats, in other words, were a divided party, not quite the "happy family" that Speaker O'Neill wanted it to be.

Not all of the defectors were ripe for Republican wooing, however. Some of the dissenters came from the liberal wing of the Democratic party and voted no because they wanted more money for social programs. The liberals usually accounted for fewer than half of the dissidents; the majority were conservative Democrats who were repelled by the high deficits and favored increased defense spending.

To win in 1981, Ronald Reagan had to persuade the conservative Democrats who were inclined to vote against their party's budget to vote for his budget, and he had to retain the cohesion shown by the Republicans in previous years. Neither task would be easy. House Democratic leaders were girding to accommodate the conservative wing, which they had neglected in the past. Representative Jim Jones (Democrat, Oklahoma), the new chairman of the Budget Committee, skillfully crafted a budget resolution that tilted to the conservatives by providing more money for defense and less for social programs. A similar tactic was used on the tax bill, with House Ways and Means Chairman Dan Rostenkowski (Democrat, Illinois) pulling out all stops to attract conservative Democrats who wanted a larger reduction in business and individual taxes.

With the outcome hanging on a few swing votes, Reagan had to do better on the Republican side than the 95 percent average attained from 1975 to 1980. If only seven or eight House Republicans had deserted the president, it might have been harder for him to corral wavering Democrats. Reagan succeeded, getting near unanimity from the Republicans and more Democrats than the minimum needed to win. But despite all the drama, arm-twisting, prime-time television, and attention given to the boll weevils, 1981 was not all that different in the House from what 1975 to 1980 had been. Ronald Reagan won because he is president, because he knows how to work the Hill and how to speak to the American people, because he threatened reprisals at the polls and promised rewards in the budget, because he had public opinion on his side and provoked a deluge of mail and telegrams from back home, because he had an extended honeymoon, and because Democratic leadership was dispirited. Others would add to this list, but it should be clear that the president had a full repertoire of political skills and resources. Yet the lessons of 1981 go beyond the behavior of one person to the leadership role of the president and to legislative-executive relations.

Beating the Democrats

From the outset, the White House had a clear vision of what it took to win. The president had to get the support of marginal members in the House (mostly conservative Democrats and moderate Republicans). He concentrated on fewer than fifty Democrats, only half of whom he needed when the votes were counted. Because the marginal Democrats were sympathetic to his cause, the president did not have to worry about alienating some of them by calling for spending cuts. He was concerned, however, about defections among the "gypsy moths," fewer than two dozen moderate Republicans who were troubled by the potential effects of the budget changes on their frostbelt districts in the Northeast and Midwest.

Most of the old-fashioned trading on the budget was with these gypsy moths, who bargained for more heating fuel assistance to the poor and elderly, for a relaxation of the proposed cap on Medicaid, and for spending increases in a few other programs. These Republicans did not drive as hard a bargain as their numbers would have allowed, for they were uneasy about abandoning the president. They could not play hardball with their own leader and they settled for less than they could have gotten.

Much has been made in the press about the favors pulled out of the bag by the president to entice the boll weevils. There were words about peanuts and sugar and about more specific promises concerning particular projects. But there was much less vote buying on the budget than the stakes might have warranted. In the end, the president won more by persuading the marginal Democrats than by buying their votes.

21

The tax bill was another matter. Here there was open vote selling and vote buying. The bargaining was tougher and more specific and involved group and individual pressures. Several factors conspired to make the outcome in the House on the tax bill a trade rather than a vote. One was the Christmas tree tradition of tax legislation; another was the determination of Democratic leaders to win at all costs; another was the confluence of different policy issues in the tax bill. Once the White House retreated from its preference for a "clean" tax bill (with all the provisions other than new depreciation schedules and changes in the basic rates deferred to a later measure), it was hard to keep at bay the armies of lawyers and lobbyists clamoring for additional tax advantages. While the spending battles provoked surprisingly little outside pressure (much less than either David Stockman or House Democratic leaders expected), the tax bill drew heavy traffic to Capitol Hill. The hogs, to paraphrase Stockman, were being fed.

Yet the leadership talents brought to the budget campaign by Ronald Reagan were of greater consequence than the material gifts bestowed upon marginal members. Reagan made a difference. Though future presidents may not possess his personal skills, they should be able to learn from his tactics.

Hard Words, Soft Voice. In demanding spending cuts, Ronald Reagan was walking into a political crossfire. Although he had been elected in a landslide and sentiment for tax and spending cuts was widespread and growing, most Americans were beneficiaries of federal largesse. Not surprisingly, therefore, over the years public opinion polls had consistently shown most Americans in favor of maintaining or increasing the spending levels for many of the programs that the president wanted to curtail. By warring against these programs, Reagan ran the risk of stirring millions of beneficiaries to active opposition. Reagan knew that he could not win in Congress if the affected interests mobilized to protect their programs. But if he soft-pedaled his economic program, he ran the risk of its running out of steam before Congress acted. He had to let Congress know that the country was on his side without incurring the wrath of mainstream America that benefited from an enlarged government.

The president's approach was to talk tough but in a soft voice. The right phrases and code words were summoned up in his televised addresses: get the government off our backs and out of our pockets; stop the black market in food stamps; eliminate fraud, waste, and abuse. If one were unable to view the president's prime-time talks but had the bare text, one would have perceived a strident president demanding drastic changes in the priorities and purposes of the federal government and a shrinkage in the welfare state built up over the previous half-century. If one actually watched the president speak, however, one heard the harsh words, but heard them delivered in a calm, reassuring manner. There was no pounding of the table, no shouting, nothing to agitate those who would be disadvantaged by the budget changes. Supporters in Congress knew what the president meant; the American people, who generally supported the president without knowing the specifics, were given little reason to be alarmed.

Mass Appeals, Personal Persuasion. The president, as just noted, had two audiences: Congress and the American people. He could not succeed in Washington if he was losing in the country. He could not attract the marginal members if the voters did not support his position.

Only a rare person is skilled both in mass appeals and in one-on-one persuasion. Ronald Reagan demonstrated that he could perform both tasks well. His television performances were great successes and brought a deluge of favorable mail, telegrams, and phone calls to congressional offices. These appearances were effectively coordinated with dozens of meetings with marginal members. Recent presidents have been too busy to "retail" their political salesmanship, preferring to deal "wholesale" with the masses or through leaders and other brokers. Reagan reminded us that if an objective is truly important for the president, he has plenty of time to pursue it. He showed that it is possible, indeed necessary, to build many bridges to Capitol Hill. Reagan met with boll weevils and with gypsy moths, with members who were already inclined to vote his way and with some who were long shots. He built a winning coalition millions of voters at a time and one member of Congress at a time.

Engaged, but Not Quite in It. Ronald Reagan had a battle on his hands, and he plunged into it with a determination to win. Yet even in battle he was above it all, never allowing himself to be fully pulled into the details or the deals. Reagan spoke in broad terms, leaving most of the hard bargaining and the specifics to others. He thus was able to do battle from the presidential pedestal, not as a combatant but as someone with superior national objectives.

This stance came through in a conversation with one of the boll weevils who succumbed to Reagan's persuasion. When I asked him what had happened in the Oval Office, he replied:

> I wasn't there more than a couple of minutes, but I didn't feel rushed and I'm not quite sure how I was shown the door. A photographer shot the usual roll of pictures; the president gave me a firm, friendly handshake. He patted me on the back

and told me how much he needed and appreciated my support. He said I should call if I need help on anything. And that was it.

I asked whether they discussed specific items in the budget. They had not.

The last time I was in the Oval Office, Jimmy Carter was there, and I came with other members to discuss a bill we were working on in committee. We had hardly got seated and Carter started lecturing us about the problems he had with one of the sections in the bill. He knew the details better than most of us, but somehow that caused more resentment than if he had left the specifics to us.

The President's Budget Maker. The main reason Ronald Reagan could avoid the details was that David Stockman was in charge of them. Stockman was ubiquitous—making deals on Capitol Hill, imposing his ideas on new and still uninformed cabinet officers, blitzing the media with facts and opinions. Reagan could have won without Stockman, but it is unlikely that he would have sought the same changes. The president probably would have settled for more modest budget objectives.

We now know that there were two budget battles in 1981. One involved Reagan and Congress; the other involved the president and his advisers. At the start, Stockman dominated both arenas, but as the year wore on, the tide turned. In not-so-private circles within the palace guard, the budget director lost on tax cuts, national defense, social security, and some lesser issues. The debilitation of David Stockman has come as much from the internal bruises as from the self-inflicted wounds in the Greider interviews. As for Ronald Reagan, he needs a restoration of harmony as much as he needs Stockman. In the future, Reagan will not be able to stay above the congressional battle if he is drawn into internecine White House squabbles.

From Dunkirk to Shangri-La. To win in 1981, Ronald Reagan had to convince Congress that economic conditions were intolerable and that the changes he was demanding would bring early and significant improvement. The president had an easy time with the first task. Economic stagnation in the 1970s brought the postwar boom to an end and propelled inflation to double-digit rates and unemployment to the highest level since the Depression. Federal expenditures tripled during the decade and big deficits became commonplace. Public opinion polls showed that Americans no longer were confident of continuing economic betterment and were worried about the future. As a presidential candidate, Reagan captured the mood of the country in the television debate with Jimmy Carter: Are you better off now, he asked rhetorically, than you were four years ago? Data showing that the real income of Americans had improved could not dissipate the feeling that things had gotten worse. David Stockman exploited this mood in his postelection Dunkirk manifesto that urged immediate action to avert an impending crisis.

For members of Congress, the economic malaise was manifested in uncontrollable spending and intractable deficits. The budget process inaugurated in 1974 had sharpened their awareness of the problem but had not given them adequate means to deal with it. In contrast to their "easy" evasion of fiscal responsibility prior to the Congressional Budget Act, members now had to vote on total spending and on the size of the deficit.[7]

Ronald Reagan told the nation that he had solutions to its economic ills and that relief would come almost immediately. He promised much higher growth and much lower inflation and unemployment than Jimmy Carter had forecast shortly before leaving office. The president supported his exuberant claims with supply-incentive explanations that justified steep tax cuts despite short-term deficits. By mid-decade, the president promised, the economy would be restored to vigor and deficits would vanish. This prescription appealed to many members who were grasping for a solution to the nation's budget and economic problems. The Democrats were unable to offer an alternative that projected dramatic economic improvement. Marginal members had to choose between the promise of economic growth and continued adversity. Understandably, many voted with the president, for the economic Shangri-La he promised, even though they had doubts about the assumptions upon which his program was based.

Voting on the President's Terms. Historically, the president has been at a disadvantage vis-à-vis Congress in their periodic budget conflicts. Congress excels as an institution that fragments issues and avoids decisions on overall objectives. Before installation of the congressional budget process, this fragmented behavior characterized legislative consideration of the president's budget. Appropriations were splintered into more than a dozen bills, tax legislation was walled off from spending decisions, and Congress did not have to vote on the totals. Members were able to profess support for the president's objectives while "nickel and diming" the budget in their action on appropriations and other spending measures. They could support a balanced budget and a reduction in total expendi-

7. Although it is common to regard members of Congress as spendthrifts who have no real interest in controlling the budget, my impression is that most members feel frustrated and helpless by the lack of effective budget control. Their willingness to use extraordinary reconciliation procedures *before* Reagan took office attests to their desire to strengthen budget controls.

tures without having to implement these widely shared objectives. The president could threaten to veto appropriations that exceeded his request, but lacking an item veto, this usually was an ineffective option. Moreover, Congress often was able to get its way by doing nothing. Since most federal spending is determined by past decisions, Congress could defeat the president by inaction.

The Congressional Budget Act strengthened the president's position by requiring Congress to vote on an overall budget policy, but actual spending decisions were made through appropriations and other measures. The act provided for a reconciliation procedure, which was used for the first time in 1980, though not as originally contemplated. Reconciliation is a procedure that compels congressional committees to report legislation conforming existing law to current budget decisions. Through reconciliation, Reagan won most of the savings he demanded by bypassing the regular authorizations and appropriations processes. The reconciliation bill that he signed was derived from instructions issued to twenty-nine House and Senate committees in the first budget resolution for fiscal 1982, and it was put into final form by a conference committee in which more than half of the members of Congress participated. This single measure produced savings estimated to exceed $100 billion during fiscal years 1982, 1983, and 1984. It covered entitlements as well as discretionary authorizations whose funding is determined in appropriation bills.

Reconciliation forced Congress to consider the budget whole and on the president's terms. More than 200 program changes were packaged into a single bill, but few of the changes were subjected to separate votes. In the House, where the decisive battles were fought, the rule under which reconciliation was considered allowed only a handful of votes on designated issues. House Democratic leaders were unable to structure the debate on a program-by-program basis. Members had to vote for or against the president's program, not for or against particular cutbacks. Reconciliation enabled the president to portray the conflict in we-versus-they terms and to avoid a discussion of specific reductions.

As a result, moderate Republicans who favored higher appropriations for certain programs than the president recommended voted for his overall policy. As already noted, without their support the president could not have prevailed. Later in the year, when specific program decisions were made in appropriations bills, many of these Republicans sided with the Democrats (see table 1). Thus, sixty-nine House Republicans voted against a floor amendment to cut the National Science Foundation appropriations; seventy-four opposed a deeper reduction in legal services funding; thirty-nine voted against a Republican effort to recommit the appropriations bill for the Departments of Labor and

TABLE 1
Votes on Appropriations Bills for Fiscal 1982

Bill	House		Senate	
	Total	Republicans	Total	Republicans
HUD	362–54	148–37	87–6	44–4
Interior	358–46	143–33	87–8	45–5
Agriculture	343–33	145–22	69–15	34–9
Energy & Water	244–104	112–44	71–22	41–8
Transportation[a]			77–15	39–11
Treasury	323–94	148–40		
State-Justice	245–145	69–104		
Labor-Health and Human Services[b]	168–249	140–39		
Defense	335–61	172–7		
Foreign aid	199–66	84–87		
First continuing resolution	281–107	90–77	47–44	40–10
Second continuing resolution	195–187	32–144		

a. The House held a voice vote on the appropriation bill for the Department of Transportation.
b. Motion to recommit.
Source: *Congressional Record.*

Health and Human Services because it exceeded the president's budget; eighteen opposed a motion to recommit the second continuing resolution that was subsequently vetoed by the president. This voting pattern also occurred in the Senate where nineteen Republicans voted to add funds for a weatherization program; twenty-five opposed a 5 percent cut in funds for the Department of the Interior; eighteen voted against an across-the-board cut in the appropriations bill for the Department of Agriculture; and nineteen opposed a similar cut in appropriations for the Department of Transportation. In many cases, Republican votes supplied the margin for defeating efforts to curtail federal spending. The motion to recommit the continuing appropriation lost by only twelve votes in the House.

Program votes do not usually follow party lines. On these votes, members are guided by program preferences, not by political ideology. If future budget votes deal with particular programs, the president might have less success than he had in the aggregated budget battles of 1981.

Controlling the Legislative Agenda. If he is not to wear out his welcome, the president cannot beleaguer Congress with too many conflicts at once. He cannot "go to the well too often" and pressure congressmen to vote against their interests and constituents. He has to be especially reserved in his demands on marginal members who tend to be cross-pressured and have to cope with conflicting loyalties.

Ronald Reagan asked a lot of Congress in 1981, but he asked it to do little. He kept his priorities clear and succeeded in spacing the major budget battles throughout the year. He did not have to yield on a budget issue to win a member's vote on another matter pending before Congress. Reagan demanded one thing from Congress at a time. When he spoke on national television, there could be no doubt as to what he wanted Congress to do. He did not clutter the legislative calendar with peripheral issues. As a conservative bent on scaling down the federal government, President Reagan did not have an ambitious legislative program; he wanted Congress to legislate less.[8]

Other than "must" legislation (such as expiring authorizations), Congress handled few nonbudget issues in 1981. There were fewer recorded votes in the House and the Senate than in any year since 1971. The number of bills signed into law by Ronald Reagan was barely half the amount enacted during Jimmy Carter's first year in office.

Despite the president's limited agenda, by the end of the year the public was less attentive than at the start, and Republicans in Congress were weary of continuous battle. They wanted compromise, not further confrontation. They had had enough of the budget and wanted to deal with other matters. Reagan's September offensive was much less successful than his earlier ones, and he got less than half of what he wanted. This partial victory was won through a presidential veto and the threat of closing down the federal government. The year ended with the president not well positioned for another round of budget battles in Congress.

The Unmaking of the Budget

Making a budget requires presidential decisions, legislative action, accurate projections, realistic assumptions, few surprises, and a cooperative economy. The unmaking of a budget is much easier. It can happen by inaction, legislative recalcitrance, economic disappointments, and events beyond immediate political control.

In recent times, the budget has been a manifestation of presidential weakness, not an instrument of presidential power. The budget appears,

8. The AWACS sale was the only truly major nonbudget issue during the session, and it was forced on the president by the legislative veto. If Reagan had had his way, the issue would not have come before Congress at all.

disappears, reappears, carried by its own momentum and not easily amenable to presidential discipline or policy changes. Recent presidents have been more successful in announcing budget policy than in implementing it. Lyndon Johnson lost his budget in Vietnam; Richard Nixon's commitment to a balanced budget was eroded by slower economic growth than he anticipated; Gerald Ford was forced to abandon his budget plans when the economy went into a tailspin during the first OPEC oil shock; Jimmy Carter remade his budget every time the economy changed course.

Inconstancy has become the hallmark of presidential budgeting. Johnson's reluctance to propose a war tax was abandoned in his belated drive for a surtax; Nixon's balanced budget doctrine was recalculated on a full-employment basis; Gerald Ford asked for a tax increase shortly after taking office and signed a tax cut only a few months later; Jimmy Carter proposed a tax rebate and then withdrew it while Congress was preparing to act. Changes made within budgets often are of greater consequence than those made between budgets. Jimmy Carter overhauled his fiscal 1981 budget less than two months after submitting it to Congress. His revision (in March 1980) called for a balanced budget; by the time the fiscal year was over, deficit spending had exceeded $50 billion.

Presidents faced with constraining budgets have practiced escapist budgeting. They try to avoid hard choices by embracing unrealistic assumptions or by asking for policy changes that they do not expect to get through Congress. After the books are closed on the budget, the failure is blamed on the economy, on Congress, or on uncontrollable forces, not on presidential illusions.

It cannot be fairly said of Ronald Reagan that he avoided tough issues. His first budget called for $45 billion less spending than Jimmy Carter asked for in his farewell budget for the same fiscal year. Reagan advocated almost $200 billion in spending reductions for fiscal years 1982 through 1984. Reagan itemized most of his reductions and fought for their enactment.

Although as of this writing Reagan's first fiscal year is barely one-quarter over, the prevailing verdict is that the outcome will be wide of the mark. Fiscal 1982 expenditures might exceed Carter's projections; the deficit will be more than twice as large. The Congressional Budget Office (CBO) sees the possibility of deficits exceeding $100 billion in 1982 and in subsequent fiscal years. One scenario projects a $160 billion deficit in fiscal 1984, the year that the budget was supposed to be balanced. Another presidential objective destined for failure is the sharp shrinkage in the relative size of the federal government. With the economy faltering and federal expenditures rising, the budget is certain to account for a significantly larger share of gross national product than the administration projected when it launched the spending-cut drive in February 1981.

Reagan's budget problems can be sorted into four overlapping categories: insufficient savings, the failure to control entitlements, faulty economic projections, and the performance of the economy.

Insufficient Savings

Despite all the attention lavished on the 1982 budget, and all the score-keeping reports and cost estimates issued by the Congressional Budget Office, no one can be certain of the amount that the president asked Congress to trim from the fiscal 1982 and later budgets or of the amount of savings enacted by Congress. Some of the reported savings actually were reestimates of Carter's budget, not policy changes; some were based on revised economic conditions; most were based on computations of what would be spent in the future if current policy were to continue in effect; some were "paper reductions" that reflected what was likely to occur even without presidential intervention. Perhaps the most enduring remark in David Stockman's revealing interview will be his admission that

> none of us really understands what's going on with all these numbers. . . . You've got so many different budgets out and so many different baselines and such complexity now in the interactive parts of the budget between policy action and the economic environment and all the internal mysteries of the budget, and there are a lot of them. People are getting from A to B and it's not clear how they are getting there.[9]

During the past several decades, the federal budget has become progressively more complex because its principal function no longer is to finance the operations and expenses of federal agencies. The budget has become a means of stabilizing the economy, redistributing income, and protecting large segments of the population against various economic conditions. When the budget merely financed federal operations, it was common for Congress to make fixed appropriations to government agencies. There was no ambiguity as to the amount by which the appropriation was higher or lower than that of the previous year. But this simple arrangement does not apply to the bulk of federal expenditures that go for income support purposes and operate as entitlements. In these programs, the amount spent in a particular year is determined by exogenous factors such as economic and demographic conditions, not by appropriations. Even where an appropriation fixes the amount

9. David Stockman in an interview with William Greider, *The Atlantic Monthly,* December 1981.

available for expenditure, the limit will have to be adjusted (through supplemental appropriations) if it is not sufficient to cover mandated expenses.

For these and similar programs, savings cannot be computed by comparing past and current appropriations. Instead, it is necessary to devise a baseline estimate and to compare spending to the baseline. This is a more complex and uncertain task than estimating fixed appropriations.

The Current-Policy Baseline. Both the Reagan administration and Congress used a current-policy baseline to compute the savings proposed and enacted in 1981. This baseline assumes that current programs will continue and adjusts their spending levels for estimated inflation and demographic changes. Suppose that a program has a current appropriation of $100 million and is expected to undergo an inflation rate of 10 percent in each of the next three years. The current-policy baseline would be $110 million for the first year, $121 million for the second year, and $133.1 million for the third year. Savings for each of these years would be subtractions from the baseline, not from current appropriations.

The current-policy approach was devised during the first years of the congressional budget process by the Senate Budget Committee in cooperation with the Congressional Budget Office. The Senate Budget Committee wanted a neutral baseline that would not be affected by presidential requests and that would enable it to distinguish between discretionary changes made by Congress and "automatic" changes resulting from past decisions, economic conditions, and other factors. Democratic members of the Budget Committee recognized another advantage in the current-policy baseline: It would be possible to "cut" the budget while increasing expenditures. If current spending were $100 million and the baseline $110 million, an allocation of $105 million would be scored as a reduction on a current-policy basis. This method helped the Budget Committee respond to conflicting pressures in Congress to cut the budget and to expand programs.

The current-policy baseline was not used by the appropriations committees, which preferred the "hard" numbers of previous appropriations and presidential requests to hypothetical baselines. The House Budget Committee worked from a baseline derived from the president's budget.

After several years of use, the current-policy baseline came under severe attack from Republicans on the Senate Budget Committee who argued that it had an expansionary bias and provided a distorted view of the committee's actions. In response, the committee moved toward a "current-law baseline" that does not adjust for inflation appropriations (such as revenue sharing) whose level is limited by law.

31

Why did Republicans on the Senate Budget Committee who, only a few years earlier, lambasted the current-policy concept as distorted and expansionary embrace this approach in 1981? And why were they joined by the Office of Management and Budget (OMB) and others who previously were reluctant to use this baseline? The simple but sufficient answer is that Republicans in both the executive and the legislative branches wanted to magnify the apparent size of the savings. The Democrats made common cause with the Republicans on this procedural issue because they wanted the actual cuts to be lower than they appeared to be. The Republicans claimed more savings and the Democrats saved more programs, a happy combination for political institutions faced with difficult choices.

Regardless of the motives for using it, the current-policy baseline is a valid, and for some purposes a technically superior, measure of changes in budget policy. It provides a common yardstick for measuring legislative and executive actions; it adjusts for the effects of inflation on services; and it removes policy changes from the baseline. Yet in the context of 1981 budget cutting, the current-policy method provided a misleading impression of the amount saved in outlays.

The Arithmetic of Budget Savings. "There was less there than met the eye," Stockman confided to Greider. "It was a significant and helpful cut from what you might call the moving track of the budget of the government, but the numbers are just out of this world. The government never would have been up at those levels in the CBO base."[10]

Regardless of how savings are computed, it is clear that Reagan got less than he asked for and that what he asked for was not all he wanted.

• The president requested a reduction of $197 billion in outlays for the fiscal years 1982 through 1984. The reconciliation bill gave him two-thirds of that amount, resulting in a shortfall of $67 billion in planned savings.

• Part of the shortfall was due to administration retreats and compromises; part to the refusal of Congress to approve proposed reductions. To win votes, the administration compromised on Amtrak and Conrail, mass transit, Medicaid, home-heating subsidies, and veterans hospitals. Congress provided more than the administration requested for the Export-Import Bank, the Legal Services Corporation, aid for the arts and humanities, and other programs.

• The administration settled for about fifty cents on the dollar in the second round of 1982 budget cuts. These reductions were pegged to the

10. Ibid.

second continuing appropriation, and some might be restored in regular appropriations bills. Several of the appropriations measures signed by the president have higher spending levels than the vetoed continuing appropriation.

• Congress has refused to act on the social security reductions, thereby adding approximately $20 billion to the 1982–1984 budget gap. The social security proposals have been put on hold and are not likely to be resurrected until after the midterm elections.

• The administration's budget projections for fiscal years 1983 and 1984 were based on the assumption that further unidentified savings of $74 billion would be requested at a later date. This "magic asterisk" was conveniently ignored during congressional consideration of the 1982 budget, but it will have to be faced in the next budget.

• An examination of the budget cuts by a team of researchers at the Woodrow Wilson School of Princeton University identified a number of "paper reductions."[11] No money was saved by placing the strategic petroleum reserve off-budget, but outlays were reduced by $3.7 billion. Pay raises for federal employees were held to 4.8 percent, leading to computed savings of almost $5 billion, even though recent pay increases have lagged behind the comparability formula established in law. Medicare payments were shifted from the first month of fiscal 1982 to the last month of fiscal 1981, with some $685 million saved by the legerdemain. Because the federal government needed $500 million less for disaster relief than had been anticipated, this amount was claimed as budget savings.

• Some of the savings achieved during the year are likely to evaporate before the books are closed on the 1982 fiscal year. Repeal of the minimum payment for social security recipients has already been scaled back by Congress. After Christmas, the president signed legislation authorizing $2.4 billion in fiscal 1982 for wastewater treatment grants, substantially more than the $40 million set in the reconciliation act. If past patterns prevail, additional spending will be provided in the supplemental appropriations bill, expected in spring 1982.

• Savings in entitlements and various grant programs depend not only on legislative action, but on the behavior of recipients and other governments as well. News reports indicate that some states have been slow to adjust to the changes made by Congress in Aid to Families with Dependent Children and other programs. Most state legislatures adjourned before the reconciliation bill became law, so that changes requiring their action have been delayed until 1982.

11. See Princeton Urban and Regional Research Center, Woodrow Wilson School of Public and International Affairs, Princeton University, "Background Material on Fiscal Year 1982 Federal Budget Reductions," December 1981.

• Many federal income security programs interact with one another; reductions in some can be partly offset by increases in others. Workers who lost their trade adjustment assistance might become eligible for welfare benefits. Some working poor who have been among the hardest hit by the federal cutbacks might leave the job market to qualify for available benefits.

The category in which the savings are firmest is appropriations for the operation of federal agencies. But, as noted earlier, this category accounts for a declining share of the federal budget, and savings of the magnitude sought by the administration cannot be realized by further reductions in these appropriations.

The Entitlement Problem

If big savings cannot come from the 15 percent of the budget that goes to federal agencies and for discretionary grants to states and localities, where can it come from? Two large and growing categories that cannot be cut are national defense, because of administration policy, and interest payments, because they cannot be directly controlled through policy changes. The administration has committed itself to high real growth in defense spending during the 1981–1986 period. Stockman lost his struggle to trim the defense increases (though small cutbacks were made), and he does not appear eager to reopen the issue. Defense now accounts for 25 percent of the budget, but its share is likely to grow since the bulk of the buildup in spending lies ahead. During the past two years, increases in budget authority have far outpaced those in outlays. This is a sure indication of steeper increases in outlays by mid-decade when payments will become due for many of the recent procurement decisions.

Interest payments, the second protected category, can be controlled indirectly through curtailment of the deficit and by successful economic management. The deficit has been rising, however, and the economy has been performing badly; as a consequence, interest costs have been rising. These costs might be as much as $20 billion above budget in fiscal 1982 and $35 billion (or more) above the administration's 1984 target.

The discretionary increase in defense and the automatic increase in interest costs will offset almost all of the real savings in 1982 and will substantially reduce the savings to be realized in future years.

The only category from which major savings can be obtained is entitlements—legal rights to payments from the Treasury. The sixty entitlement programs account for approximately half of the budget, but the Reagan administration has protected some of the largest, the "Main Street" entitlements, in its "social safety net." The favored programs include the basic social security coverage, unemployment assistance, veterans benefits, and Medicare. Some savings were secured in these (provoking critics to charge that the safety net had holes in it), but the bulk of the entitlement reductions were concentrated in programs for low-income families such as Medicaid, food stamps (technically not an entitlement, though it has the basic characteristics of one), and Aid to Families with Dependent Children.

The administration's failure to constrain Main Street entitlements seriously weakened its drive for cutbacks. The day after the March 1981 budget was unvēiled, economist Michael Evans in the *New York Times* stated that "the failure to come to grips with . . . indexation and entitlements calls into question the commitment of the Reagan team to sweeping, broad-based budget cuts. . . . His nickel and dime approach is unlikely to have the desired effect of bringing government spending to heel."

Actually, the administration made two efforts to curb entitlements. In the spring, it "floated" some far-reaching changes in social security benefits, but subsequently disowned (without quite withdrawing) them when Democrats and Republicans attacked them. The president has repeatedly indicated that social security will not be a target in the next round of budget cuts. The second effort came in September 1981 when the president announced that "in the near future" he would propose $26 billion in entitlement savings for fiscal years 1982 through 1984. When congressional Republicans informed the White House that they did not want to tackle the entitlement problem in the closing weeks of the session, the proposed reforms were deferred to the 1983 budget.

Entitlements pose financial and political difficulties for the president. They constitute the bulk of uncontrollable spending, and most are open-ended. Together with interest payments, they account for almost all of the unbudgeted rise in federal spending during the fiscal year. The president makes the budget; entitlements unmake it. Further, when he makes the budget, the president is hostage to past entitlement decisions; most of the year-to-year rise in spending is locked into entitlements that grow apace with inflation and demographic changes.

Reagan's advisers are aware that the president cannot master the federal budget unless he controls the growth in entitlements. The administration, however, has not devised a political strategy for tackling the problem. The tactics that work so well for reducing discretionary expenditures backfire when they are applied to entitlements. The administration bested Congress by confrontation; it cannot win that way with entitlements. The affected interests are too big, too vigilant, too mobilized. For them, a loss in benefits translates into a loss in take-home pay, and they can be expected to fight for their rights.

35

To make significant changes in entitlements—especially in social security—requires consensus between the White House and Capitol Hill and between Republicans and Democrats. Reducing entitlements cannot be a partisan, we-versus-they issue for the simple reason that the president cannot possibly bring spending under control without the support of marginal Democrats and moderate Republicans.

Consensus on reductions in entitlements is not easy to obtain in the best of circumstances; in 1981, it was impossible. The White House learned that it cannot confront the Democrats on the budget and expect their cooperation on social security. To cope with its entitlement problem, the administration will have to adopt a budget strategy different from the one it used in 1981.

Faulty Economic Projections

A budget is a projection, not a contract. It is based on expectations about the future, and its objectives can be attained only to the extent that the expectations are realized. When federal budgeting was a self-contained process for financing the expenditures of government agencies, the principal uncertainty was what Congress would do to the budget. Nowadays, however, the unknowns relate to the performance of the economy and to the behavior of recipients. As economic growth has become less assured and predictable, the reliability of budget projections has declined. This problem has beset all recent presidents, but none as much as Ronald Reagan.

It is politically difficult for a president to publish best-guess projections about the future course of the economy. To project rising prices or higher unemployment is to pronounce one's budget policy a failure. Economic forecasts are congenitally optimistic; they project the next year to be better than the current one, and each future year to be more favorable than the one preceding it. Unemployment and inflation will abate, economic growth will be vigorous, interest rates will decline. With these projections, it is easy to promise a balanced budget, not right away, but within a few years.

Since 1975, each budget has contained five-year outlooks for prices and jobs. Over this period, there have been seventy such projections, all but a handful of which have shown year-to-year improvement. Of course, when the next budget is issued, the rolling projections are revised to show higher levels of inflation and unemployment than was foreseen a year earlier.

CBO issues its own economic projections, which, though nominally independent of the executive's projections, are inevitably influenced by them. CBO cannot be completely realistic if OMB is not; it cannot pre-

TABLE 2

Presidents' Economic Assumptions for Unemployment and Inflation Rates, Calendar Years 1975–1986

Year Economic Assumptions Were Made	1975	1976	1977	1978	1979	1980	1981	1982	1983	1984	1985	1986
Unemployment (annual average)												
1975	8.1	7.9	7.5	6.9	6.2	5.5						
1976		7.7	6.9	6.4	5.8	5.2	4.9					
1977			7.3	6.6	5.7	4.9	4.8	4.7				
1978				6.3	5.9	5.4	5.0	4.5	4.1			
1979					6.0	6.2	5.7	4.9	4.2	4.0		
1980						7.0	7.4	6.8	5.9	5.1	4.3	
1981 [a]							7.8	7.2	6.6	6.4	6.0	5.6
Inflation rate (annual change in CPI)												
1975	11.3	7.8	6.6	5.2	4.1	4.0						
1976		6.3	6.0	5.9	5.0	4.2	4.0					
1977			5.1	5.4	5.0	4.6	3.8	2.9				
1978				5.9	6.1	5.7	5.2	4.7	4.2			
1979					8.2	6.7	5.7	4.5	3.4	2.7		
1980						11.8	9.2	8.2	7.4	6.8	6.1	
1981 [a]							11.1	8.3	6.2	5.5	4.7	4.2

NOTE: Economic assumptions were made in January for each of the years shown.
a. 1981 assumptions are those issued by President Reagan in February, not Carter's January estimates.
SOURCE: Congressional Budget Office.

dict that the economy will deteriorate when the president says it will get better. CBO appears to position its projections so that they are a bit more forthright than the administration's, but they are not necessarily CBO's best guess of what will happen.

In composing their fiscal 1982 projections, Reagan's advisers vacillated between euphoria and trepidation. On the one hand, Stockman and his aides quickly realized that future deficits might be worse than they had feared; on the other hand, supply-siders in the administration expected the new tax policies to trigger sustained economic growth. We now know that OMB manipulated its econometric model to obtain the expansive projections published in the budget. It justified this action with the argument that existing models could not accommodate the changes that the administration's economic recovery program would generate. Its projections for fiscal years 1981 through 1986 were much more favorable than those Carter issued one month earlier. Inflation would be cut by two-thirds; two points would be shaved off the unemployment rate; real growth would average 4.4 percent a year; interest rates (on three-month Treasury bills) would be halved. This was the Shangri-La that helped sell the Reagan program. (See table 2.)

The projections came under immediate attack from mainstream economists who argued that the assumptions were inconsistent. If expansion would be as vigorous as forecast, inflation would be higher and so too would interest rates. Some feared that the steep tax reductions would fuel a new round of inflation; some doubted that high growth could be sustained for such an extended period. It now appears that the economy is doing better than forecast only with respect to inflation; interest rates and unemployment are worse, and the economy is experiencing recession rather than expansion. Perversely, inflation is the only one of these indicators where improvement adds to the deficit. Table 3, drawn from a recent CBO report, displays the estimated impact of variances from economic projections on the budget deficit. Note that the effects grow in the outyears; a small shortfall in economic growth adds a little to the deficit in the first year but snowballs into a much larger deficit three to four years later.

The recent horror stories about prospective deficits in fiscal 1982 and beyond are primarily due to expected deviations from the economic projections issued by the administration when it came into office. Yet, unrealistic projections have more than a passive effect on the budget; they encourage budget makers to avoid difficult issues. Why consider whether the United States really can afford to lower taxes while raising defense expenditures when an expanding economy will satisfy both objectives? Why take on the short-term financing problems of the social security system when they will be solved by economic growth? Why

38

TABLE 3

EFFECT OF ONE-PERCENTAGE-POINT VARIANCE FROM 1982
PROJECTIONS ON FY 1982–1986 BUDGET DEFICITS
(billions of dollars)

Economic Indicator	Change in the Budget Deficit for Fiscal Year				
	1982	1983	1984	1985	1986
Real economic growth	8	17	33	47	66
Inflation	−4	−11	−19	−33	−49
Unemployment	19	28	30	33	35
Interest rates	2	4	5	6	7

NOTE: Table shows the amount the budget deficit would increase or decrease
(−) if in calendar 1982 an economic indicator is one percentage point worse
than was assumed in the first budget resolution for FY 1982.
SOURCE: Congressional Budget Office, *Baseline Budget Projections, Fiscal Years
1982-1986.*

resist efforts to load additional revenue-losing provisions onto the tax bill
when future revenues will soar because of favorable economic conditions?

Budgetary escapism feeds on itself as decisions are taken (or
avoided) that ensure future deficits, ill-timed fiscal policies, and a continuing upward creep in the relative size of the federal sector.

Performance of the Economy

Ronald Reagan gambled with the economy in 1981; the preliminary
verdict is that he lost. It could be that the current recession will prove
to be shallow and short-lived, and that once tax reductions take effect
the economy will boom again. It is highly unlikely, however, that the
targets announced in February 1981 will be realized.

Before examining the reasons for failure, it is appropriate to consider why the administration ventured so boldly in the economic arena.
It is not merely that supply-siders captured key posts and enticed the
president with visions of economic plenty. Ronald Reagan tried a new
line because neither Keynesian prescriptions nor conventional budget
balancing offered acceptable solutions.

During the heyday of the "New Economics" in the early 1960s,
Keynesians were confident that the budget could be used to stabilize the
economy without high inflation or unemployment. In the 1970s, however, the belief that the budget can shape the economy yielded to the
frustrating notion that the economy shapes the budget. Economic adversity yields lower receipts and higher expenditures than were budgeted

and transfers resources from the private to the public sector. Moreover, the perverse combination of unemployment and inflation—stagflation—weakens the capacity and the will of the government to restore economic health. If the government tries to dampen inflation by exercising fiscal restraint, unemployment worsens before inflation abates, and budgetary discipline is abandoned before it has a chance to work.

The Reagan administration was determined to reverse the relationship between the budget and the economy. Rather than the budget nurturing the economy to vigor, the economy would restore the budget to balance. The president was convinced that the budget could not be controlled as long as stagflation persisted. Even in the face of a fiscal 1982 deficit acknowledged to be $45 billion, a conservative Republican decided to cut federal taxes. To break the economy's stranglehold on the budget, the president gambled that future growth would take care of the deficit.

The Reagan administration demonstrated in 1981 that having three economic theories is not better than having only one, especially when each theory focuses on a single aspect of economic behavior. The supply-siders cared about marginal tax rates and incentives to produce, to save, and to invest; they were not alarmed by the size of the deficit. Neither were the monetarists whose first priority was to mitigate inflation by restricting the growth in the money supply. The "deficitists" were a medley of old-fashioned conservatives who worried about any red ink and new conservatives who worried about excessive deficits.

Because each theory had its proponents in the administration, the easiest way to work out internal differences was to cordon off one policy area from another. It was for this reason that, in Stockman's words, "the pieces were moving on independent tracks." The supply-siders got tax cuts; the deficitists got spending reductions; the monetarists got low money growth. Actually, with all the squabbling among insiders, no one got all that he wanted. In a concession to the deficitists, the tax reduction was deferred for three months; the spending reductions were less than they would have been if the supply-siders had really campaigned for them; and the monetarists got mixed signals, with White House spokesmen both lauding and attacking the Federal Reserve's restrictive policy.

The price of these internal fissures was contradictory economic policy. Monetary restraint clashed with fiscal expansionism, producing soaring interest rates and a sharp downturn in the economy. The monetary targets could not support the economic targets. This contradiction, pointed out by Rudolph Penner shortly after the Reagan budget was issued, has continued to plague administration policy.

The fractures in the administration's economic thinking are likely to deepen as the economy deteriorates and deficits escalate. Supply-siders will feel vindicated in their belief that tax relief should be accelerated; the monetarists will see evidence that the federal government cannot discipline itself and that monetary restraint is the only long-term hope for curing inflation and other economic ills; the deficitists will campaign for a new round of savings because the first round did not cut deep enough.

It should be fascinating to see whether the administration fights more with itself in 1982 than with Congress.

Can Political Success Coexist with Economic Adversity?

The budget no longer will be held hostage to the economy, David Stockman declared at the dawn of the Reagan presidency. It now appears that not only will the budget be held hostage but so too will the administration. Its political resources will be dissipated if the economy continues on a sluggish course over the next few years.

If the Shangri-La scenario were to materialize, however, the political problem would take care of itself. If inflation moderates, job opportunities improve, real incomes rise, and interest rates stay down, the president will have his way with Congress. Not only would he have strong public support, but his budget problem will be easier if high growth produces less spending and lower deficits.

Because of the contradictions mentioned above, I do not expect the rosy scenario to unfold. The administration has already sown the seeds of its future with economic and budgetary difficulties. Steep tax cuts will cause the rise in federal revenues to lag behind the rise in federal spending. In the face of massive deficits, the Federal Reserve will be tempted to reimpose monetary restrictiveness, and a new spiral in interest rates will begin.

Regardless of the medium-term performance of the economy, recovery will not come fast enough to help the president in his next round of budget battles. The signs point to another large package of savings in the fiscal 1983 budget and fresh confrontations with Congress. On the basis of last year's performance and the president's political talents and resources, one should be wary of betting against him the next time. But the odds now are against a replay of 1981 in 1982.

Republicans and Democrats in Congress are weary of budgetary conflict; the more intractable the problems seem to be, the less they want to tackle them. They are tired of having their broader legislative interests crowded out by never-ending budget crises, and they do not want to have every issue denominated in budgetary terms. Members are resentful of the concentration of power and of legislative activity forced

41

by the 1981 reconciliation procedures, and they do not want this to become a recurring feature of the legislative process.

In 1982, members will be looking back to presidential performance and ahead to congressional elections. They will have a record on which to judge the president's budget, not just the promises of a new administration. They will be cautious of new budgetary entanglements that might endanger their support at the polls. They might impose further cutbacks on programs that have weak clients, but these will add up to smaller savings than were enacted in 1981. They do not expect the president to repeat his wizardry in front of television cameras, and they suspect that America is growing bored with budgetary matters. They expect the news media to give increased attention to the hardships caused by budget cuts and to the redistributive features of the president's program. They also expect the president to be more distracted by international events in 1982 and, like other recent presidents, to become less interested in budget issues as his administration matures.

Moderate Republicans and marginal Democrats are most likely to desert the bandwagon or to exact higher prices for remaining on board. In November, the president had difficulty holding them on the continuing resolution, and in December a group wrote him urging him not to target certain programs for curtailment in 1982.

It could be that the president will be more interested in political confrontation than in budgetary success, that as his economic troubles deepen he will seek to pass the blame to Congress. He, too, will be looking ahead to future elections, and he might try to get the support from voters that he cannot get from legislators.

There is an alternative interpretation of presidential behavior, which, if valid, would require a rewriting of this paper, beginning with its opening line. Ronald Reagan's battle in 1981 was not really against the federal budget or against the deficit. His target was an active, meddling federal government that got into matters it should not have, that espoused values he was opposed to, and that supported causes contrary to his convictions. The president had a hit list of federal programs, and the budget was his instrument for eliminating them. He did not like the war on poverty or a meddlesome legal services program; he was against the Comprehensive Education and Training Act and federal intervention in the arts and humanities. He would rather have a smaller government with a bigger deficit than a bigger government with a smaller deficit. He would rather have the government spend more as long as it did less (in the domestic arena). He was not against helping the poor but really believed that they would do better by casting their lot with an expanding economy than with an expanding bureaucracy.

42

Bits and pieces of support for this interpretation can be gleaned from presidential behavior in 1981. William Greider's article reveals that Reagan was informed of the future deficit problem and of the improbability of his controlling spending without controlling entitlements. He also must have known that future increases in defense spending combined with steep tax cuts would ensure expanding deficits. Most of his retreats on proposed cutbacks were in programs with which he had no ideological quarrel.

Maybe Ronald Reagan did win in 1981. He did not get the budget he professed to want, but perhaps the budget was only a cover for his real objectives. Some of the programs he did not like were curtailed; a few were eliminated. In 1982, he can take fresh aim at his hit list while using the budget to mobilize support for spending control. He will not get rid of the deficit, but he might get rid of more disliked programs.

Congressional Liaison in the Reagan White House: A Preliminary Assessment of the First Year

Stephen J. Wayne

Introduction

By all accounts, Ronald Reagan's relations with Congress have been remarkably successful. When judged by the performance of his three most recent predecessors, he appears to have accomplished herculean tasks. It is necessary to go back to Lyndon Johnson to find a president who received similar support for his major legislative proposals during his first year in office. In view of the significant institutional and political changes that have occurred in presidential-congressional relations since Johnson's time, Reagan's achievements are that much more impressive.

What were the ingredients in his success? Who was primarily responsible—the president, his legislative strategists, his operatives on Capitol Hill, or the Republican leadership in Congress? This paper tries to answer these questions. It does so by contrasting this administration's congressional relations with those of previous administrations. The structure and operation of Reagan's congressional liaison office, the strategy and tactics that it has employed in Congress, and the roles of the president and his principal aides in legislative activities are described and assessed. A projection of the problems that lie ahead is also foolishly attempted. First, however, a brief history of presidential liaison with Congress is presented.

The Institutionalization of Congressional Liaison

In order to exercise their constitutionally designated legislative functions—to report on the state of the union, to recommend necessary and expedient legislation, to summon Congress into special session, and to approve or negate enrolled bills and resolutions—presidents have always had ongoing dealings with Congress. As these functions have been

44

expanded, so have presidential interest and involvement in the legislative process. Much of the involvement has become institutionalized, particularly in the post–World War II era. The presentation of an annual program to Congress, the coordination of that program within the executive branch, the drafting of legislation, and the submission of special messages are now standard fare. Within the presidency, structures and processes have been created to help perform these functions.

At the beginning of the Eisenhower administration, another role was formally acknowledged: the advocacy of presidential proposals in Congress by the president's agents. Another staff was created to perform it: the White House congressional liaison office. Modeled after General Marshall's army liaison office during the war, its initial task was to explain the president's programs to the Republican-controlled Congress. After 1954, when the Democrats regained the majority, it assumed an additional responsibility: to prevent legislation opposed by the president from being enacted into law. Eisenhower's agents maintained a low profile and assumed a bipartisan approach on Capitol Hill. They worked primarily through the congressional leadership. Their style was to nudge rather than to twist arms.

With the election of John F. Kennedy in 1960, the scope of congressional liaison was expanded, and the operating style of the office changed as well. In addition to pushing White House initiatives, the president's liaison team began funneling legislative views into the executive decision-making process. The increasing development of policy by the White House made this input desirable from a congressional perspective.

Under the direction of Lawrence J. O'Brien, the office maintained a more visible, more partisan approach than it had during the Eisenhower era. Greater pressures were exerted on Congress by the White House. Attempts were made to organize department and agency liaison staffs more effectively behind the administration's priorities. In an effort to improve the atmosphere for the administration on Capitol Hill and to meet an increasing need of Congress, the White House liaison office began to provide casework services for members and their staffs. This care and feeding operation soon became a congressional expectation, one that subsequent White Houses could not shirk. Social lobbying increased as well.

It is difficult to assess the impact of these expanded activities on presidential influence in Congress. Together they undoubtedly contributed to Johnson's successes. Helped by the huge Democratic majority in the 1964–1968 period, the incubation of policy initiatives "whose time had come," the momentum generated by the Kennedy assassination, and his own skills as a legislator, Johnson succeeded in getting Congress to enact most of his Great Society programs.

Richard Nixon and Gerald Ford were less successful in inscribing their legislative stamp on Congress. Their partisan and ideological differences with the Democratic Congress seriously affected their ability to build coalitions behind their policy objectives. These differences suggest the limits of what a liaison staff can do for a president.

Both presidents had capable liaison staffs. They were about the same size as they had been in the Kennedy-Johnson period. Staffed by Capitol Hill professionals, they performed what had come to be regarded as traditional liaison activities: gathering intelligence, influencing votes, channeling information, and serving constituency needs.

There were, however, some structural differences within the White House hierarchy that adversely affected the ability of the congressional liaison office to deal with Congress, particularly during the Nixon administration. William Timmons, operational head of liaison during much of this period, reported through a legislative counselor to the chief of staff, who reported to the president. The distance to Nixon reduced Timmons's stature in the eyes of Congress. Nixon's own inaccessibility, not only to members of Congress but to his own staff, further aggravated the problem.

Ford's liaison head also reported through a chief of staff to the president, but neither Donald Rumsfeld nor Richard Cheney, who held the position, impeded access to their president as Haldeman and Haig had done for theirs. Ford remained open to and popular with legislators. He was one of them. Ironically, that may have been one of his difficulties. His longtime service in the House of Representatives combined with the manner in which he became president made it difficult for some members of Congress to see him as presidential. His friends in Congress still called him Jerry. His stature suffered.

The Nixon and Ford experiences demonstrate the impact of partisanship and, to a lesser extent, ideology on presidential-congressional relations. They also indicate that personal considerations do affect how a president gets along with Congress. But these factors alone do not account for all the problems these presidents had. Significant political and institutional changes occurring during the 1970s made it more difficult for any president to influence Congress. These changes included the weakening of parties, the growth of single-interest groups, the evolution of a subcommittee system, the expansion of legislative staffs, and the reassertion of congressional authority in reaction to the excesses of Johnson and Nixon. Camouflaged by the partisan and ideological differences between the Republican presidents and their Democratic Congresses, the impact of these developments did not become apparent until the presidency of Jimmy Carter. Some believe that Carter and his liaison chief, Frank Moore, were among the last to learn of them.

Carter and Congress

Jimmy Carter was not a very effective legislator. This perception, shaped by memories of Lyndon Johnson and expectations of Democratic leadership, was shared by Congress and the public alike.[1] The White House congressional liaison office took much of the blame for Carter's difficulties. Frank Moore, the fellow Georgian whom Carter appointed to head the office, lacked congressional experience. Hampered by an understaffed transition liaison operation, a new and untested Democratic leadership, and very unrealistic expectations by Democratic members of Congress, Moore got off on the wrong foot and never recovered.

The initial problem was twofold: Moore's inexperience in dealing with Congress and Congress's overeagerness to deal with the administration. Designated as Carter's personal representative, Moore came to Washington in July 1976. He was quickly inundated with phone calls, messages, and requests for appointments. Some phone calls were not returned, some messages were lost, and some appointments were missed. Criticism of Moore, though muffled by the campaign, began to emerge after Carter's victory. The beginning of the congressional session three weeks before the inauguration further complicated the new liaison chief's tasks. "When we came into this office on the 21st, we got 1,100 letters from members of Congress in our first week on the Hill," he stated.[2]

The expectations of Democrats in Congress clearly exceeded the administration's capacity to fulfill them. "Sixty percent of the Congress had never dealt with a Democratic White House, so they didn't have realities in mind," suggested a top liaison official in an interview. "They looked for a rubber stamp White House. It was a learning process on both sides of the street."

Nonetheless, during the course of the administration, the congressional liaison office made significant adjustments in its operation, gained experienced personnel, and achieved a reasonable degree of success for the president's program. Its reputation, however, did not improve.

By the spring of 1978, the liaison staff had increased to forty-one despite the highly publicized reduction of the overall White House staff by 30 percent. Much of that increase was in support staff to aid in execu-

1. A survey of members of Congress conducted by *U.S. News and World Report* in 1977 found that only 7 percent rated Carter as very effective with Congress. In contrast, Reagan was evaluated as very effective by 93 percent of those responding to a similar survey by the magazine four years later. Courtney R. Sheldon, "How Reagan Rates with Congress," *U.S. News and World Report,* October 12, 1981, p. 27.

2. Frank Moore as quoted in Spencer Rich, "Shakedown Cruise," *Washington Post,* February 25, 1977, p. A2.

tive branch coordination and casework. Internal task forces on key initiatives were formed to coordinate the administration's congressional activities. A mechanism for setting priorities for highly visible issues was established. Headed by the vice president, its job was to identify and schedule vital legislative initiatives. More sophisticated information retrieval systems and computerized mail logs were developed to process congressional mail and assess voting patterns. Even the president, a private person by nature, began to interact more frequently with members of Congress, particularly the leadership. There were more White House social events for legislators of both parties.

The quality of personnel also improved. William Cable, brought in to head the operation in the House of Representatives, enjoyed a solid reputation from the outset, and Dan C. Tate, the chief Senate lobbyist, gained in stature. Robert Thomson, who became Moore's deputy, tightened the internal workings of the office and eventually chaired the early morning deputies' meeting at the White House.

In conjunction with these changes in the staffing and operation of congressional liaison, other presidential offices got more involved with Congress and the legislative process. The domestic policy staff, although it did not solicit congressional views, became more receptive to them. Members of Congress and their staffs were given opportunities to affect the development of proposed legislation before it was sent to Congress.

Most impressive was the creation and development of the public liaison office. Established in April 1977 under the direction of Anne Wexler, it functioned as an integral part of Carter's effort to influence Congress. An outreach program involving elaborate White House briefings for interest group and community leaders and for local media was conducted on a continuing basis for the last two-and-one-half years of the administration. It consumed more of the president's time than any other White House activity.

The objective of the outreach program was to organize groups and prominent persons into a coalition behind important administration proposals. Self-interest and self-interest alone was the attraction to join. Once established, the coalition, orchestrated by the White House, mounted grass-roots efforts and carried out selected liaison activities.

The mechanism for exerting influence was essentially the same. Liaison representatives from the White House and interest groups would target members of Congress. Prominent persons within their constituencies would be asked to communicate directly with them. Letter-writing campaigns would also be organized. The goal, to demonstrate constituency support for the president's policies, was designed to make it easier for Democrats to vote with the administration.

As a consequence of all these efforts—the outreach program, more effective congressional liaison, greater involvement by members of Congress in presidential policy making, a more experienced and skilled Democratic leadership in Congress—the administration scored some notable legislative successes: the creation of two new executive departments (Energy and Education), airline and trucking deregulation, civil service reform, the Alaska Lands Bill, multilateral trade agreements, and Senate ratification of the Panama Canal Treaty. George C. Edwards III, a political scientist, found that Jimmy Carter's support in Congress almost rivaled that of Lyndon Johnson; in fact, Carter enjoyed greater support from Senate Democrats, equal support from Senate Republicans, and slightly less support from House Democrats and Republicans.[3]

Despite these policy successes and the high support scores he received, Carter's image as a legislator did not improve significantly during his administration. Nor did that of his liaison chief, Frank Moore. This suggests that reputations created at the outset may persist and have a lasting effect on an administration's ability to get its way with Congress.

What were the initial errors that affected Carter's relations with Congress? First, he appointed as head of his congressional liaison staff an inexperienced man who did not appreciate the amenities and courtesies due members of Congress. Second, the administration did not take advantage of the honeymoon period: too much legislation was introduced too late. Third, priorities were not effectively established; the administration's position vacillated on several of its so-called key proposals.

Moreover, Carter provided legislators with few incentives for following his lead. His anti-Washington, anti-"politics as usual" stance was viewed as naive at best and offensive at worst by members of the congressional community. Finally, the president's style detracted from his efforts. His knowledge of the issues was impressive, but his all-business style won him few converts or permanent friends. The Reagan team did not want to repeat these mistakes.

The Reagan Transition

Carter's congressional problems had begun during the transition. In contrast, Reagan's congressional transition was smooth and efficient. A separate transition liaison office, headed by an experienced congressional lobbyist, Tom Korologos, and consisting of eleven professionals including two former White House congressional aides, was established immediately

3. It must also be pointed out that Edwards analyzed only the first two years of the Carter administration. His statistics are based on presidential support scores as calculated by the *Congressional Quarterly*. The score represents a legislator's voting agreement with the president on all those votes in which the administration has taken a position. There is no attempt to evaluate importance or impact of the votes. George C. Edwards III, *Presidential Influence in Congress* (San Francisco: W. H. Freeman, 1980), pp. 190-96.

49

after the election. Every member of the staff had some Capitol Hill experience.

The liaison office operated throughout the transition period, during the postelection session of the Ninety-sixth Congress and the first three weeks of the Ninety-seventh. It had three major functions: to provide ongoing liaison for the president-elect; to schedule meetings for him with members of Congress during his pre-inaugural visits to Washington; and to help in the confirmation of the cabinet. Each of these functions was essential.

Without its policy established or its structure in place, the new administration did not want to be hamstrung by legislation enacted during Carter's final months in office. "Don't let them do violence to us" was Korologos's message to congressional Republicans during the postelection session. "You know these bills better than we do."[4]

In addition to protecting its flank, the Reagan team wished to ingratiate itself with members of both parties in the new Congress. Its principal ingratiating instrument was Reagan himself. As a candidate he had gone out of his way to show solidarity with congressional Republicans. A media event, staged on the steps of the Capitol, provided him with a convenient backdrop to call for the election of a Republican Congress. "Don't send me to Washington alone," he urged voters.

Once elected, he met with Republican leaders and gave them a voice in cabinet and subcabinet selection. "We had to lasso him to keep him off the Hill," Korologos noted.[5] In addition to Reagan's activities, his transition liaison office maintained channels of communication with Congress, particularly with the Republicans.

An avalanche of congressional phone calls and mail quickly followed Reagan's victory. Most of the correspondence, requests for jobs for constituents, was funneled to the personnel office. The volume of letters, over 25,000, overwhelmed the transition staff, with the result that boxes of unanswered correspondence were shipped to the White House after the inauguration. "It took us several months to catch up," stated Charlotte Ponticelli, director of congressional correspondence for the new administration.[6]

The designation of Max Friedersdorf in December 1980 to head the White House congressional liaison office provided seven weeks for start-up activities.[7] Freed of transition liaison responsibilities, Friedersdorf could

4. Tom Korologos, interview, November 10, 1981.

5. Ibid.

6. Charlotte Ponticelli, interview, November 5, 1981.

7. Korologos had been offered the job but refused for personal reasons. "I had done it before," he noted. So had Friedersdorf, who was chief White House liaison for the House of Representatives from 1973 to 1974 and headed the entire office during the final years of the Ford administration, 1975-1976.

concentrate on staffing his office and on influencing the selection of department and agency liaison officials. During December and early January, Friedersdorf and Korologos worked closely together on these appointments. They had been deluged with résumés from Congress, estimated by Korologos at around 500.

During this period, two other decisions were made: to retain as many slots as possible for White House congressional liaison in the new administration and to move the office from the Old Executive Office Building to the East Wing, where it had been housed before the Carter administration. Both decisions had symbolic importance. They testified to the high priority attached by the Reagan administration to congressional relations. Korologos commented: "The EOB is not the White House. In this town images mean a lot. The Hill saw congressional liaison go back in the White House. They saw the pros go in. To that extent we tried to do what Carter didn't." [8]

In hiring his own staff, Friedersdorf enjoyed complete discretion. He also exercised a major influence in the selection of the department and agency liaison heads. The Reagan administration, determined not to repeat Carter's error of allowing cabinet secretaries to choose their own liaison assistants, even retained a veto of lower-level appointments in the agencies. [9]

Moreover, the word was passed that offices of congressional liaison were to be integrated into department and agency operating structures. They were to be apprised of all congressional contact by their other divisions. In this way it was hoped that the political appointees who held the top liaison posts could monitor, intercept, and generally inhibit contact by civil servants that threatened to undercut the administration.

These actions enabled the new team to get a running start with the Congress. In place two weeks before inauguration, the White House congressional liaison staff began making visits to Capitol Hill, serving members of Congress, and observing amenities immediately after the inauguration. Phone calls from members of Congress were returned promptly (usually within four hours), and all correspondence was to be acknowledged. "If you take care of the little things, the big things will take care of themselves," Korologos stated. [10]

In addition, the president had bipartisan leadership breakfasts at the White House, met with key Senate and House Republicans, and even invited Speaker Thomas P. (Tip) O'Neill to two private dinners in the

8. Korologos, interview.

9. Political appointees constitute approximately one-third of those involved in agency liaison activities.

10. Korologos as quoted in Elizabeth Wehr, "Reagan's Team on the Hill Getting Members' Praise for Hard Work, Experience," *Congressional Quarterly*, May 2, 1981, p. 747.

White House—a far cry from the treatment O'Neill had received at the beginning of the Carter presidency.

These efforts bore fruit. Congressional liaison received high grades. The *Washington Post* headlined its first assessment of the operation "Reagan Hill Team Gets Rave Reviews."[11] Other accolades followed. The victories were to come.

Structure and Operation

The congressional liaison office under Friedersdorf did not differ markedly from its predecessors, particularly its Republican predecessors. Somewhat smaller than Carter's, it included twelve professionals in a total staff of twenty-seven. There were the traditional House and Senate liaison assistants and a correspondence section.

Unlike their counterparts in the Carter office, the president's special assistants in the House and Senate were not initially subdivided along geographic or policy lines.[12] The intention, according to John Dressendorfer, one of the House lobbyists, "was to have all members of the staff accessible and responsible to all members of Congress."[13] In time, however, loose jurisdictional areas did develop along policy lines, the special assistants tending to deal with certain legislators and their staffs more or less regularly.

Coordination within the office was loose and informal. Staff meetings were held daily from Monday through Friday. Arriving around 7:30 A.M., liaison aides normally met with their chiefs for the House and Senate, Kenneth Duberstein and Powell Moore, at separate but adjoining tables in the White House mess at 8:00 A.M. A representative from the liaison staff of the Office of Management and Budget (OMB) usually participated. Before these breakfast meetings, Duberstein and Moore would consult with Friedersdorf, and at least one of the White House special assistants would attend the OMB legislative staff meeting at 7:30 A.M. The purpose of the early morning meetings was to plan congressional activities for the day. Discussion centered on the congressional calendar. It was at these sessions that the assignment of responsibilities— who would contact whom—was made.

11. Helen Dewar and Lee Lescaze, "Reagan Hill Team Gets Rave Reviews," *Washington Post,* March 17, 1981, p. A5.

12. At the beginning of the Carter presidency, House lobbyists were given responsibility for specific issue areas. When Cable took over the House operation, he reassigned his four special assistants to specific state delegations, and these assignments held for the remainder of the administration. The Senate staff consisted of only two, Dan Tate and an assistant, who covered the entire body.

13. John Dressendorfer, interview, November 5, 1981.

Concurrently, at 8:00 A.M., Friedersdorf attended the senior staff meeting in the White House. Afterward, he reported to the entire liaison staff. By 9:00 A.M. aides were at work in the White House; by 10:00 A.M. they were on Capitol Hill, where they remained for the day. Contact with the White House was maintained through a beeper system. No specific Capitol Hill office was used. Phone calls were returned and casework was performed in the late afternoon and early evening. Social events often followed, and the day ended at anytime from 7:30 P.M. to 9:00 P.M.

Friedersdorf supervised office activities. He functioned as an administrative chief, legislative tactician, and trouble-shooter. He was the link to the senior staff and participated with James Baker, Michael Deaver, and Ed Meese in the morning meetings with the president when legislative matters were discussed. "I spend more time with him [Reagan] than I do with my wife," Friedersdorf quipped.[14]

Coordination with department and agency liaison was handled by William J. Gribbin, Friedersdorf's deputy. It too tended to be informal. At the beginning of the administration, meetings were conducted with the department and agency liaison heads, but these were subsequently discontinued. The only regular contact the department and agency liaison heads had with the White House was through their written reports, which were submitted on Friday. The reports included a synopsis of the week's congressional activities and a forecast for the coming week. They were made available to all professionals in the White House congressional liaison office and to the other outreach offices. They were *not,* however, distributed to other department and agency liaison offices.

Executive branch agencies were expected to take the lead on their own programs, including major presidential initiatives. For the budget battle, the OMB took the lead; for the tax cut, the Treasury Department took the lead on the numbers and the OMB on the policy; for the AWACS sale, the State Department handled liaison activities until the final weeks, when the White House mustered a major effort; the Department of Agriculture led on the farm bill.

Generally speaking, the White House liaison office did not become involved unless there was a discernible presidential interest. According to Sherrie Cooksey, special assistant for liaison in the Senate, "We try to limit the number of issues to three per week."[15]

Although departments and agencies exercised discretion on their own issues, that discretion might be limited by the interests of the administra-

14. Max Friedersdorf, "Remarks to the National Capital Area Political Science Association," December 4, 1981.

15. Sherrie Cooksey, interview, November 23, 1981.

tion. In addition to clearing their positions, programs, and testimony with the OMB, agencies were expected not to divert congressional attention during major White House policy pushes.[16]

For major priorities of the administration, overall strategy was set by a White House group consisting of Baker, Deaver, Meese, the outreach directors, and relevant cabinet officers.[17] Meeting frequently in Baker's office, the legislative strategy group was charged with coordinating congressional activities. Baker, unlike his counterparts in the Carter administration, was intimately involved in this process.

Below the senior level, however, the coordination of legislative strategy tended to be free-form at best. Cabinet councils that formulated interagency policy did not generally become involved in planning how to get that policy enacted on Capitol Hill. The economic cabinet council was an exception. Some work groups were involved in mapping and coordinating legislative strategies for their own efforts, but their involvement stemmed more from the initiative of an individual staffer than from any regularized, action-forcing process. In the words of one White House aide I interviewed who participated in such an endeavor, "In this administration, unless someone decides to take the ball and run with it, nothing is likely to get done."

One of the primary objectives of the strategy group that operated out of Baker's office was to tie the outreach activities to the congressional liaison operation. The administration put considerable effort into organizing the grass roots behind the administration's major goals. The public liaison office was in charge of the nuts and bolts. While the congressional liaison office benefited from these activities, it was usually not directly involved in them and might not even be informed of them. Visits and communications to members of Congress by groups and their supporters supplemented the contacts the president and his aides made.

The Reagan administration depended primarily on the organization of business groups and trade associations for much of its outreach effort. Over a thousand such groups supported the administration's budget and tax proposals. Intelligence from these groups was funneled informally into the congressional liaison operation; there was no regular reporting system.

The public liaison office organized telephone banks before important presidential speeches. It arranged for special briefings by the president and his top aides for its friends. "Before the president goes on television,"

16. Federal grant and contract announcements are made by the appropriate department or agency, not by the White House as in previous administrations.

17. The outreach directors in 1981 were Richard S. Williamson (intergovernmental affairs), Max Friedersdorf (legislative affairs), Lyn Nofziger (political affairs), Elizabeth Dole (public liaison), and David Gergen (communications).

one liaison official noted in an interview, "we first bring in our allies. He meets with them in private—several hundred at a time. He gives them an advance view of what he is going to do so that they can alert their allies to be prepared to go." These activities helped to create the flood of telephone calls that the White House and members of Congress received after the president's addresses to the nation on his budget and tax proposals.

The office of political affairs, headed by Lyn Nofziger in 1981, was also involved in the congressional process, particularly on personnel matters. With political clearance one of its primary responsibilities, the office had frequent contact with Republican legislators, particularly in the Senate, who sponsored candidates for positions. The liaison staff did the legwork on potential presidential nominees. It passed résumés from Congress to the White House personnel office, lobbied for some choices of key Republican senators, alerted the White House to possible trouble for others, and helped smooth the way for the administration's eventual choice.

During the first months of the Reagan presidency, most congressional letters to the White House concerned personnel matters. Later, although candidates for positions were still being urged, congressional interest turned more to policy issues and constituency needs. The volume of mail from Congress also subsided somewhat, averaging thirty-five to fifty pieces per day in the fall of 1981.

The correspondence was processed in much the same manner as during the Carter period. Incoming presidential mail was logged into a computer, and a daily summary of each communication was prepared for the president. Reagan usually commented on most items. Infrequently, he asked to see a letter and dictated a specific response.

Most policy-oriented mail was sent to the appropriate agency after being logged. The congressional liaison office usually received a draft of the agency's reply before it was sent. All requests for administration positions are cleared by the OMB.

The congressional liaison office also handled a large volume of case mail that was forwarded to the White House from members of Congress. This mail included requests for presidential pictures, testimonials, and meetings, opinions of constituents, and requests for a variety of services. All this correspondence was acknowledged except for insulting or threatening letters, which might be turned over to the Secret Service.

Most telephone calls were handled like letters. A phone call by a member of Congress to the president was usually referred to an appropriate House or Senate aide, whose job was to inquire into the purpose of the call and either handle it himself or, if need be, arrange for a telephone appointment with the president. The staff aide was also responsible for preparing the president's talking paper in the event of such a call. The congressional leadership could normally reach the president directly through his appointments secretary.

As in previous administrations, the congressional correspondence unit initiated mail on major presidential initiatives as well as the more routine thank-you and congratulatory notes, invitations, and other "personal-like" correspondence. For the routine as well as the important mail, the end was the same: to improve the atmosphere for the president on Capitol Hill.

Legislative Strategy and Tactics

In designing its approach to Congress, the Reagan administration adopted certain strategic principles. Rooted in the failures and successes of past administrations, these principles constituted the game plan for the first year.

The foremost component of this plan was control of the agenda. The previous administration, in particular, suffered in Congress from the "too much, too late" syndrome. By promoting a wide range of social and economic policies, Carter found it difficult to control the congressional calendar, focus the media, and mobilize support for his programs. The lesson was clear: the fewer the initiatives, the easier the coordination and the greater the time that could be spent on building congressional majorities.

Reagan's legislative strategists understood the lesson well. "The president was determined not to clutter up the landscape with extraneous legislation," Friedersdorf stated.[18] His campaign rhetoric—government was too large and costly, taxes were too high, defense was too weak, and regulations were too numerous—translated into two basic legislative initiatives, budget and tax reform, and two basic executive ones, a hiring freeze and a reduction of regulations. Two other legislative issues, the AWACS sale and the farm bill, were essentially forced on the administration.[19] These four issues constituted the administration's entire agenda for Congress for 1981. They monopolized the calendar. Congress did little else.

Moreover, the administration was able to schedule the issues in such a way as to maximize support from members of both parties. By con-

18. Friedersdorf, "Remarks."

19. The current farm authorization was due to expire, and a new bill was needed. Farm authorizations extend for four years. Congress had enacted a veto provision in its legislation dealing with military assistance. The sale of AWACS planes to the Saudis was subject to this provision. The administration, of course, was aware of this as well as of the opposition to the sale. It chose to ignore that opposition, however, until after the tax vote. By then the potential legislative veto had become a referendum on the president's foreign policy in the Middle East.

centrating first on the budget, then on taxes, then on the AWACS sale, and finally on the farm bill, Reagan used the honeymoon period to great advantage and maintained the momentum from his election victory for almost nine months.

Since the budget and tax proposals involved major changes in spending priorities and taxing structures, the administration believed it essential that they be considered and enacted early. Reagan strategists gave themselves six months. "We knew we had to get our bills enacted before the Labor Day recess," Friedersdorf said.[20] His reasoning was straightforward: over time partisan divisions reemerge, and presidential popularity declines; Congress becomes more receptive to constituency interests and pressures and less able to legislate with a view to the national interest. This decreases the chances of getting innovative policies enacted.[21]

Acting at a time when the desire for unity and his own popularity were greatest, Reagan made a national appeal for support of his economic programs. He couched it in nonpartisan terms, thereby placing the onus of self-interest on would-be opponents. This compounded the difficulties that those out of power face in articulating a position and generating support for it. The skill with which Reagan and others in the administration made this appeal, combined with the lack of a real policy debate, helped overcome the tendency of Congress to be parochial on budget matters. By the fall of 1981 parochialism had returned, but not before the initial budget requests had been accepted and the tax cuts enacted in a form acceptable to the administration. After some posturing and a veto of a continuing budget resolution, a compromise on the administration's revised budget won approval.

Moving early and quickly on domestic economic matters, those that are apt to be most divisive, served another purpose. It took advantage of the unity of the Republican party and the disarray of the Democrats. The lack of articulate Democratic spokesmen and, above all, strong House leadership provided the administration with a splendid opportunity to use its leverage to build winning coalitions in both houses.

The congressional liaison office relied on Howard Baker's leadership in the Senate to produce a partisan majority. They concentrated their efforts almost entirely on the House for the budget and tax votes. This concentration naturally helped Robert Michel, the new minority leader, to hold the Republicans in line. His success was vital to the administration's efforts.

20. Friedersdorf, "Remarks."

21. A strong partisan bond between the president and Congress might overcome this tendency, as it did during much of the Johnson presidency. Obviously, such a bond was not present between the White House and the House of Representatives in 1981.

To woo the necessary Democrats, the administration adopted a two-pronged strategy aimed primarily at conservative Democrats, particularly those from districts that Reagan had carried overwhelmingly in 1980. One part of the strategy consisted of a private, low-keyed appeal by the president at the White House or Camp David. The other part of the strategy was to use the "bully pulpit." This gave the president an opportunity to exhibit his communicative skills and flex his muscles.

Reagan's two television appearances before critical roll calls on the budget and tax proposals produced a huge grass-roots response. This spontaneous outpouring, generated by the president and magnified by his administration's outreach efforts, provided designated Democrats (and others) with the excuse they needed to vote for the administration's bill and remain in sympathy with the people who had elected them.

Although public support was a major dimension of the administration's strategy, it was not the only dimension. "Politics as usual" was not totally suspended; the administration remained politically sensitive. It made deals when necessary. Writing in the *New York Times Magazine,* Hedrick Smith listed some of the deals: "White House backing for a sugar price-support, more funds for Medicaid, Conrail, energy subsidies for the poor, or a slow-down on mandatory conversion to coal for industrial boilers in oil-producing states." [22] Ward Sinclair and Peter Behr of the *Washington Post* described many of the same trades: "The high-level horse-trading for Democratic votes included concessions by Reagan on sugar price-support legislation, federal aid for Conrail, reduced aid for the poor, student loans and the Clinch River fast breeder reactor in Tennessee, among other items." [23] In a much-quoted statement, Representative John B. Breaux (Democrat, Louisiana) said, "I went with the best deal." When asked if his vote could be bought, Breaux replied, "No, it can be rented." [24]

Not surprisingly, congressional liaison aides were reluctant to discuss this aspect of their relations with Congress. "There is not as much horse-trading as you have been led to believe," Powell Moore stated. "We don't say, If you give us this, we will give you that. But we *do* try to cooperate with them." [25]

Trading was always referred to as taking place somewhere else. "There is more of that in the House than in the Senate," Moore stated. [26]

22. Hedrick Smith, "Taking Charge of Congress," *New York Times Magazine,* August 9, 1981, p. 17.

23. Ward Sinclair and Peter Behr, "Horse-trading," *Washington Post,* June 27, 1981, p. A1.

24. Ibid.

25. Powell Moore, interview, November 5, 1981.

26. Ibid.

Another congressional assistant commented: "We are not in a position to do that [trade]. We make contact with members. If there is some receptivity, if we think that member can be convinced and if we cannot do it on our own, we get word to the powers that be."[27]

If deals were made, they could be authorized by only a few senior aides: Baker, Meese, Stockman, and, in some cases, Friedersdorf. The president was careful to avoid making promises when communicating with members of Congress. His style was to listen and to indicate that their concerns would receive consideration.

Part of the strategy to maximize flexibility, minimize leaks, and present a unified position was to limit public discourse by and to a few administrative officials. Middle- and lower-level White House aides were discouraged from talking on the record. Interviews were difficult for reporters and political scientists to obtain. This magnified the president's voice and those of his senior aides and reduced discordant notes within the administration.

Reagan's willingness to involve himself in legislative activities was instrumental to the success of the administration's efforts. According to Friedersdorf, the president spent more time on congressional affairs than on any other aspect of his responsibilities.[28] Before each pivotal vote, he met with key members and saw or called the fence sitters.

His style contributed to his effectiveness. He used a soft sell. Citing basic arguments and illustrating them with a few statistics, he would ask for support and then answer questions. He was always affable; his demeanor was presidential. "Reagan's a charmer," boasted one of his aides. "He radiates confidence. He is very good on a personal basis with members." The contrast with his predecessor was striking.

The only persistent criticism of Reagan the lobbyist had concerned the depth of his knowledge of the issues. Speaker O'Neill publicly chided the president for demonstrating less detailed information on the budget than any other president he had observed while in Congress. Robert Michel, the House Republican leader, commented to much the same effect: "Sometimes I think, my gosh, he ought to be better posted. Where are his briefing papers?"[29]

Yet even this lack of specificity may be part of the strategy. In addition to being consistent with Reagan's personal style, it reduces his burden and, most important, his risk. Verbal blunders, poor judgment, and costly errors can be and have been blamed on subordinates. The president avoids responsibility and ridicule by not having been informed about the

27. Dressendorfer, interview.
28. Friedersdorf, "Remarks."
29. Robert Michel as quoted in Smith, "Taking Charge of Congress," p. 47.

details. All accomplishments, of course, result from his leadership. Eisenhower followed a similar strategy with great success.

Although the liaison chief, Friedersdorf, maintained a low profile in dealing with Congress, his style and manner were also praised. "Smooth," "low-keyed," and "unflappable" are some of the adjectives used to describe him. Even though his credentials were strongly partisan, Friedersdorf made few enemies on either side of the aisle. His reputation contrasted sharply with that of his Democratic predecessor, Frank Moore.

Assessment and Projection

By almost any standard, Reagan's first year with Congress must be judged a success. He got the legislation he wanted: his initial budget requests and many of his second-round reductions, his tax bill with most of its major components intact, and a farm bill he could accept. The sale of AWACS planes to Saudi Arabia was not stymied by a legislative veto, nor was the confirmation of Sandra O'Connor to the Supreme Court derailed by conservative opposition. Moreover, Reagan prevented legislation he did not want from being seriously considered, and he created an atmosphere conducive to his future success. "The foundation of good congressional relations will remain through this term and another one, if there is another term," predicted Friedersdorf confidently.[30]

There were some mistakes and a few instances of poor judgment: several nominations had to be withdrawn; the AWACS sale unnecessarily snowballed into a foreign policy referendum; the administration had to revise its budget estimates and restrict its social security proposals. But these failings paled in comparison with the accomplishments.

Why was the administration so successful? Three reasons stand out: (1) it limited and controlled the congressional calendar; (2) it effectively performed its liaison activities; (3) it exercised skillful personal leadership. Each of these was critical.

Control of the agenda obviated the need for other priority-setting mechanisms. It muted the expectations of the right and thereby removed diversions from the congressional calendar. It appealed to and helped build a broad coalition of Republican and conservative Democrats behind the president's proposals.

By limiting and staggering the issues, the administration was able to set the pace and influence the tenor of the debate. It was able to insert the president most expeditiously into the legislative decision-making process. It was also able to focus public attention more clearly on certain

30. Friedersdorf, "Remarks."

presidential activities and foster the impression that Reagan was in command.

Shaping the public's perception of what Reagan was doing and how well he was doing it served another purpose: it credited him with the fruits of victory. This, in turn, contributed to his popularity and, if Richard Neustadt is correct, to his persuasiveness with members of Congress and made future victories more likely. The administration operated on the principle that chips are gained, not lost, by playing them.

Finally, control of the agenda enabled Reagan to overcome what had been perceived at least in Washington as a major stylistic and perhaps cognitive deficiency: his presumed inability to consider multiple issues in depth at the same time. With an issue-by-issue approach, Reagan could immerse himself in "the policy of the month" or, more precisely, of every other month. Members of Congress were pleasantly surprised by his knowledge (the three-by-five index cards notwithstanding) as well as charmed by his personality. This combination proved far more enticing than Carter's all-business expertise.

There is, of course, a reverse side to a limited policy agenda. Some expectations will not be satisfied; some problems will not be solved. For the Reagan administration it was the social agenda of the conservatives that was postponed. Being a Republican, having a narrower constituency, contributed to Reagan's ability to focus on economic matters. Moreover, the opposition of many of his supporters to government involvement in general created a less favorable climate in which to develop and propose other domestic initiatives. It was not accidental that the office of policy development in the White House maintained a low profile and a limited output.

A Democratic president, even a conservative one, would have had a much more difficult time constraining his agenda. Carter found this out the hard way. How long social issues could be kept off the congressional calendar and whether the administration could keep its hands off social issues were uncertain. Acknowledging this problem, Powell Moore stated: "It will be harder to control the agenda as time goes on. Issues will converge at the wrong time. A lot [of our success] has to do with our ability to control our own destiny. We have been lucky so far."[31]

The congressional liaison office was more than lucky. By starting early, recognizing congressional needs, and effectively catering to them, the office was able to gather intelligence and peddle influence for the president without seeming to offend the sensitivities of Congress or intrude on its legislative prerogatives. The importance of liaison during the transition and the first months of the new administration cannot be overesti-

31. Moore, interview.

mated. This is the time when campaign debts are due, when personnel requests threaten to overwhelm Congress, when the president appears to have all the perquisites, when the uncertainties of channels of communication and patterns of influence are greatest. Under the circumstances, small favors are apt to be remembered; later on they are taken for granted.

Once under way, the operation of the liaison office was not very different from that of Carter. Friedersdorf's staff was a little less structured and much less systematic in its coordination than congressional liaison had been in the previous administration, at least in its final two years. In the short run, this looser, more informal operation proved to be an advantage. It enabled the liaison agents to get to know more members more quickly. Not burdened with numerous meetings and reports, the president's people had more time to spend in the halls of Congress. Moreover, the limited agenda minimized fallout from multiple activities that were not precisely coordinated. It also allowed a small group of senior staffers to oversee the entire process from priority setting to strategic planning to tactical operations.

All the problems lay ahead. As an administration loses its ability to control the congressional calendar, interagency coordination becomes much more important. Coalition building becomes more difficult; resources are spread thin. The senior staff cannot orchestrate the entire show.

Lack of coordination has already become apparent. "What causes me a great deal of frustration on my job," said one liaison aide, "is when I find out that I did not receive a copy of something." Complained a White House official: "On nonbudget matters, the only way to move things is to do it yourself. There is no action-forcing mechanism." Another assistant in one of the policy-making units commented sadly, "There is no decision-making process in this administration. Groups are formed, decisions are made, and then the next week the issue is thrashed out again. What has surprised me most is the amorphousness of power here."

If White House lines of authority are blurred, if interagency coordination is not systematically extended into the legislative area, if turnover increases among liaison aides, if the senior staff becomes preoccupied with nonlegislative matters, the administration is in for trouble. The problem is particularly acute among the twenty-six department and agency liaison offices, staffed by almost 600 political appointees and civil servants. Coordination difficulties surfaced between the White House and the departments of Agriculture, Energy, Housing and Urban Development, and State and the Environmental Protection Agency.[32] Greater strains ap-

32. Bill Keller, "Executive Agency Lobbyists Mastering the Difficult Art of 'Congressional Liaison,'" *Congressional Quarterly,* December 5, 1981, p. 2392.

peared likely unless internal decision making and coordination were improved.

The third ingredient in the administration's legislative success has been personal leadership: the president's communicative talents and interactive style, his chief lieutenants' organizing skills and liaison activities, and Senator Baker's and Representative Michel's vote-counting and courting abilities. Together these individuals created a team that outmanuevered and overwhelmed congressional Democrats.

Reagan merits much of the credit. His ability to elicit public and private support became a distinguishing feature of his presidency. One has to go back to Kennedy to find another chief executive with a similar combination of lucidity and charisma and to Eisenhower to find as commanding a presence in the White House.

Reagan has benefited enormously from comparison with his predecessors. The assessments of them enhanced his image and contributed to his ability to exercise leadership. The perception of Ford and Carter as weak and ineffective has helped fuel the desire for a stronger, more assertive president, with a well-defined sense of himself and his goals.[33] Reagan's personality, his style, and the way he clearly focused and articulated his policy initiatives helped tailor his image to the public's ideal.

Reagan's strengths, absent in previous presidents, filled a great need. The ability to mobilize public support—to trigger the grass-roots organizations throughout the country—has become essential to the building of policy majorities. With Congress more decentralized, with partisan ties weaker, with the legislative process more public, with members more susceptible to outside pressures, private persuasion needs to be reinforced by public support disaggregated on a constituency basis. This has been Reagan's forte.

His weakness—a lack of detailed knowledge on a multitude of issues—has not hurt him. On the contrary, it has helped to shield him from the lapses and foul-ups of his subordinates. Bloodletting has occurred at a lower level; the president has been protected.

There is danger ahead, of course. Too much discretion exercised by subordinates can limit the options and influence of those at the top. It can also create dependency, real or imagined, and a tendency to cling too long to advisers who get into trouble. Carter suffered from his failure to cut his connection with Bert Lance when Lance's past became an issue, and Eisenhower suffered from his inability to break with Sherman Adams.

33. Responses to an identical Gallup poll question asked in 1976 and in 1979 revealed that 14 percent more of the respondents in 1979 favored strong leadership and were less fearful that such leadership might be dangerous. Stephen J. Wayne, "Expectations of the President," in Doris Graber, ed., *The President and the Public* (Philadelphia: Institute for the Study of Human Issues, forthcoming).

Reagan has avoided thus far being hurt by his advisers' many problems, but how long he can continue to do so is uncertain. The effect of his age, his workload, the complexity of issues, and internal disagreement on his future relations with his staff is also difficult to foresee.

The involvement of the president's chief of staff has elevated the importance of legislative activities to the highest priority. It has made the administration's cues easy to follow. It has also helped remove problems of access to the top on the key issues.

Friedersdorf's position on the senior staff, his frequent contact with the president, and his ability to speak for the administration on Capitol Hill enhanced his status in the eyes of Congress and discouraged end runs around him. Only Howard Baker, Robert Michel, and Tip O'Neill seemed to have a direct line to the Oval Office.

Finally, Baker's and Michel's leadership were impressive. Their ability to maintain a majority in the Senate and remarkable unity among Republicans in the House lessened the administration's task of achieving winning coalitions and acceptable conference reports.

Would this personalized style of leadership continue to be as effective after the first year? Would the president's appeal wear thin? Might a proliferation of issues, including some unexpected ones, make him appear less competent? Would the inevitable clashes and losses in Congress seriously detract from his mystique and impair his ability to mobilize future support?

What would happen if the economic program were not successful or continued to be a subject of heated debate? How would this affect the public's perception of the president and his popularity? Could it transform his image from one of assertiveness into one of inflexibility? Might it raise questions about his competence and that of his advisers? Would it undercut his credibility or make further adjustments both necessary and more difficult? At the very least, the approach of the 1982 congressional elections would increase the partisan identities of House Democrats and thereby make the building of a majority coalition in the lower chamber more difficult.

In addition to programmatic and partisan considerations, there were the usual exigencies of time and effort. Would other issues inevitably divert Reagan's and Jim Baker's attention and sap their energies? Would the furious pace of White House liaison continue to take its toll? Would Ken Duberstein, who replaced Friedersdorf in 1982, be as effective as Friedersdorf, not only on Capitol Hill but in the White House?

Legislative affairs are an inevitable mix of people and institutions, of personalities and processes. The administration's tendency to rely on a small group of very senior officials was made possible only by its concentration on a few issues, albeit issues that were complex in character and broad in impact. The question remained, however, Could the administration exercise as much control over the legislative agenda in 1982, 1983, and 1984 as it did in 1981? Could it continue to keep the legislative objectives of others from diverting its goals or co-opting its resources? Signs were already apparent that the scope of the administration's efforts would shrink, not expand, in the year ahead.

A return to "normalcy" in contemporary presidential-congressional relations would increase conflict and decrease cooperation. If this happened, the administration's priorities would be affected. Legislative affairs would become less important as they became more difficult. More effort would be directed toward other goals.

For congressional liaison, the task would remain the same even though the work became harder and more tedious. Bermuda sojourns would be likely to increase.

Reagan, Congress, and Foreign Policy in 1981

I. M. Destler

Congress is a reactive body, particularly in a president's first year. This gives any new administration a certain initiative. When that administration wins power by an impressive electoral margin, it has a basic choice about how to exploit that initiative. It can press quickly for maximum policy change to fulfill the mandate it claims from the electorate. Or it can proceed with caution, granting some continuity with its predecessor, seeking modest policy change with bipartisan support.

The Reagan administration opted clearly for the first course. On economic policy, it pressed for deep budget and tax cuts, waged the sort of coordinated policy-political campaign that Capitol Hill had not seen for many years, and won major statutory changes by the August recess. On foreign policy also it promised fundamental departures: a rearming America was going to show long-overdue toughness toward the Soviet Union and its proxies, bringing new strength to our alliances, building strategic consensus in the Middle East, drawing a firm line in Central America. Yet its early congressional record on foreign policy was anything but impressive. By the time of that same August recess, the administration was under attack over El Salvador, stalemated on foreign aid, and stumbling into a costly uphill struggle to keep Congress from blocking airplane sales to Saudi Arabia.

In the second half of 1981 the administration became, out of necessity, more pragmatic, more modest in its goals, more willing to compromise on means. It also became more successful—not only salvaging the AWACS (airborne warning and control system) sale but winning the first regular foreign aid appropriations in three years. In the conclusion of this essay I argue that the pragmatism and the success were related. But first, a selective review of Reagan, Congress, and foreign policy in 1981.

A Mandate for Toughness

When he entered office, Ronald Reagan could properly claim electoral mandates on both economic and foreign policy. The economic mandate was at once stronger and less specific than the foreign policy mandate. The electorate voted against stagflation and high interest rates and in favor of a new approach, but there is little evidence that public opinion favored what became Reagan's specific economic program: large, "supply-side" tax cuts, tight money, and the Stockman budget reductions.

Foreign policy was probably less crucial to the electoral outcome. Although voters were wary of war, a trend of several years, accentuated by Afghanistan, toward support of the military and a tougher international posture seems to have continued. Thus the Reagan mandate on foreign policy, while lower on the scale of voter concerns, had clearer direction and content.

This swing to the "right" on foreign policy, toward what Tom Hughes has labeled the "security culture,"[1] was consistent with the direction in which Congress had been heading since the mid-1970s. In 1979 the Senate had both resisted Carter's SALT II treaty and used it as a lever to extract increased defense spending commitments. In 1980 Congress had been reluctant to press its claims for involvement—the object of great struggle in the 1970s—when Carter unilaterally decreed a new Persian Gulf doctrine in January and launched an unsuccessful hostage rescue operation in April. It had granted the president somewhat greater foreign policy flexibility in the foreign assistance authorization act enacted in December.

The 1980 election brought, of course, a sharp further shift in the same direction—the surprising Republican capture of the Senate and gain of thirty-three seats in the House. Thus, unlike Nixon and Ford, who faced resistance from the left, and Carter, who was assaulted from the right, Reagan had a Congress in basic ideological harmony with his views. Finally, the new Senate was without most of the leaders of the revolution of the 1970s—Jacob K. Javits (Republican, New York), Frank Church (Democrat, Idaho), Clifford P. Case (Republican, New Jersey), Hubert H. Humphrey (Democrat, Minnesota), J. William Fulbright (Democrat, Arkansas), John C. Culver (Democrat, Iowa), George McGovern (Democrat, South Dakota), and Dick Clark (Democrat, Iowa). Only three members of the Foreign Relations Committee had been on the committee as recently as five years before.

There was thus reason to believe Congress would be responsive to the sharp foreign policy departures Reagan was promising. Yet the

1. Thomas L. Hughes, "The Crack-Up," *Foreign Policy* (Fall 1980), pp. 33-36.

reforms of the 1970s endured: the Congress remained open, fragmented, decentralized, and therefore hard for anybody to manage. The foreign policy committees, through which bills and nominations would move, were substantially to the left of their parent bodies. The Senate Foreign Relations Committee had added six new moderate-to-liberal members. The House Foreign Affairs Committee had awarded chairmanships of regional subcommittees to activist liberals—Lee H. Hamilton (Democrat, Indiana), Stephen J. Solarz (Democrat, New York), Howard Wolpe (Democrat, Michigan), Michael D. Barnes (Democrat, Maryland)—who would be quick to challenge administration policy around the globe.

January–July: A Shaky Start

Congress reflected the mood of toughness in its early endorsement of large shifts of money from domestic programs to defense. But on foreign policy issues the administration's rhetoric frequently had the unintended effect of energizing those on the other side of the ideological divide. When the secretary of state drew the line in El Salvador, the most immediate effect was to arouse those who were reluctant, as in Vietnam, to commit American prestige and lives to the resolution of a morally messy conflict in an obscure small country. Public and congressional reaction was so wary that on March 24 the administration nearly lost a symbolic test vote in the House Foreign Operations Subcommittee on reprogramming $5 million in military aid funds. Representatives Jamie L. Whitten (Democrat, Mississippi), chairman of the full committee, and Silvio O. Conte of Massachusetts, the ranking Republican, had to be brought in to cast ballots ex officio so the administration could scrape by, 8 to 7. The White House got the message: El Salvador was unpopular, and it distracted attention from the top-priority economic program. So the rhetoric was cooled. Nonetheless, Congress responded by tacking onto aid legislation restrictions that tied our continued assistance to progress in human rights and to economic and political reforms.

The administration's determination to lean strongly to the right also got it into trouble on nominations. Secretary of State Alexander Haig came strongly through his marathon confirmation hearings, despite some difficult passages, and won overwhelming (93–6) Senate endorsement. The California judge William P. Clark fared much worse after he failed the current events test of Senator Joseph R. Biden, Jr. (Democrat, Delaware), receiving twenty-four negative votes on his nomination as deputy secretary, though he subsequently gained respect as a critical link between the Haig State Department and the Reagan White House. More damaging to administration-Senate relations, however, were the

Ernest W. Lefever debacle and the protracted difficulties on State Department regional and economic appointments.

The position of assistant secretary of state for human rights and humanitarian affairs, created at the initiative of Congress, had substantial symbolic importance if limited real power. Lefever, a prolific, idiosyncratic, neoconservative scholar with a divinity degree, proved to be a triply vulnerable nominee: he had spoken in opposition to governmental involvement in human rights issues overseas; his research institute had engaged in questionable funding practices; and he proved, in the words of one close observer, "a terrible witness—his own worst enemy." He blamed "Communists" for the opposition to his nomination, for example, and then denied doing so. As one administration official put it, "every time you send him down to meet a senator, you lose a vote." Human rights advocates, by opposing him, were able to build the maximum impression of strength for their cause. But because Lefever was seen by Reagan's conservative coalition as a committed "true believer," it was hard for the administration to back off the nomination without seeming to betray both its values and its people.

So the administration did the opposite, raising the stakes just as Lefever's support in Congress was disintegrating. Determined not to lose, particularly to those perceived as Reagan's ideological adversaries, the White House took over from the State Department the responsibility for lobbying for the nomination, invited Lefever to a forty-minute, publicized session with top Reagan aides, and engaged in political hardball with Chairman Charles Percy of the Foreign Relations Committee, who had been trying to get the nomination withdrawn. Reagan's political aide Lyn Nofziger led the public attack, but his chief of staff, James Baker, was said to be active as well. Among the steps they took were delaying a choice by Percy for U.S. attorney, leaking damaging material (apparently) to columnists Evans and Novak, and excluding Percy from the delegation to Cardinal Wyszynski's funeral in Poland. The result was to stiffen Percy's opposition, and when the committee acted, the four new Republican members joined him in the 13 to 4 negative vote on June 5. Later that day, Lefever was persuaded to withdraw.

In contrast to its ill-advised toughness on Lefever, however, the Reagan White House was notably reluctant to fight its right-wing ally, Senator Jesse Helms (Republican, North Carolina), on several mainstream State Department nominations. At issue were six conservative-to-moderate men with established experience and expertise—Myer Rashish, Lawrence Eagleburger, John Holdridge, Chester Crocker, Robert Hormats, and Thomas Enders—who had been named to important regional and economic posts, most as assistant secretaries. Helms had remarkably little Senate support in his fight against them:

not one of his colleagues on the Foreign Relations Committee voted against any of the six in committee, and ultimately only eleven negative notes (four on Rashish, seven on Crocker) were cast on the Senate floor. Although Haig had proposed most of these nominations in January, it was May and June before they were finally approved. In the meantime, the designees "lived in sin," as one later put it, occupying the offices and doing the jobs anyway—draining some of the substance from the confirmation process. At least two of them—Crocker and Holdridge —were manifestly damaged, though Eagleburger may have gained credibility when he got Helms to abandon his opposition without visibly compromising himself.

The common tendency was to blame Percy for failure to stand up to Helms—"a terminal case of political meekness" is how *Time* described it[2]—and this charge was echoed widely in the executive branch and on Capitol Hill. Percy had delayed a vote on Crocker, though his staff attributes the delay to scheduling problems. A look at the relevant dates, however, suggests that the prime causes of delay were elsewhere: (1) overelaborate review procedures, involving collection of extensive personal and financial data first by the administration and then by the committee, and (2) the reluctance of the White House and Senate Majority Leader Howard Baker (Republican, Tennessee) to challenge Helms directly. The Crocker nomination, for example, was not submitted by the White House until two months after Haig proposed it; and after the Foreign Relations Committee endorsed it 16 to 0, with Helms absent, Baker allowed it to languish on the executive calendar for forty-one days before bringing it to a vote!

Eventually, Helms was the formal loser—all six were confirmed, he apparently extracted little in return, and his lengthy, sometimes comical questionnaires to the nominees held him up to some ridicule. But Helms showed how vulnerable a divided administration was to his purposive assaults, and he managed to make the committee and the Senate leadership look weak as well. Later in the year, his demonstrated troublemaking capacity would give the still struggling Haig pause when contemplating Holdridge's replacement by a man Helms found objectionable.

Repeatedly in its early months, the Reagan administration came across as overcommitted to its causes and to the ideologues in its camp, while misreading how foreign policy issues were actually playing on Capitol Hill. Such misreading was particularly acute on the AWACS issue, which is addressed at length in the next section. One cause of difficulty was the explicit decision to give priority to the economic program. The widely praised White House Legislative Affairs Office

2. *Time,* May 7, 1981, p. 20.

under Max Friedersdorf had no in-house foreign policy expertise and—more important—showed little interest or accomplishment in foreign policy. White House relations with Percy had been rocky ever since he had overreached himself on a postelection trip to Moscow and the Reagan transition staff had leaked a politically damaging cable reporting his endorsement of an Arafat-led Palestinian state. Chairman Percy's determined, evident, sometimes maladroit efforts to nudge the administration toward a more centrist, bipartisan approach on such issues as arms control proved a further irritant. Public wrangling between Secretary Haig and the White House "troika" was yet another source of difficulty: not only was the Reagan inner circle neglecting international issues, but it felt unable to give the State Department a mandate to fill the gap. On foreign assistance, State Department officials had already obtained endorsement of significant statutory changes from the Senate and, to a lesser degree, the House committees, but it was uncertain whether the White House would give this unpopular legislation the commitment and priority its approval would require.

The Reagan congressional performance on foreign policy did improve, however, in the second half of 1981. The AWACS sale was rescued; a priority-shifting foreign assistance package was enacted. This resulted in part from an explicit summer decision to give international matters greater presidential priority. It also reflected a significant turn toward the center—toward pragmatism, even some bipartisanship. Ironically, this progress came over the same period that the Reagan-Weinberger defense plans began to generate serious doubts, and congressional support for Reagan's economic policies began to disintegrate.

Reagan and AWACS: An Issue He Never Made

From January through September, the Reagan administration threatened to make the proposed sale of advanced radar aircraft to Saudi Arabia into a textbook case of how not to manage a politically volatile foreign policy issue. First, the air force was allowed to continue the negotiations with the Saudis, already well advanced in the Carter administration, to the point where an up-or-down White House decision was required, without exploring such obvious options as NATO-like joint ownership and management and before the administration had had time to work out its broader policy and political priorities. Second, the White House decided to plunge ahead, as recommended by the Defense Department, which laughably estimated only thirty-five senators in opposition, disregarding the far more realistic, and pessimistic, State Department prognosis and undercutting the secretary of state, who had been working out Israeli agreement to a different approach: F-15 enhancement immediately, the AWACS deferred. Belatedly realizing that there might be a serious political problem, the administration accepted Senator Baker's recommendation that formal notification be deferred until detailed arrangements were reached with the Saudis. But simultaneously the White House made its third serious mistake—barring administration officials from arguing the substantive case on Capitol Hill. They could urge legislators to remain uncommitted and promise that "when you finally hear our case, you'll like it," but no more. Thus they ceded the substantive battlefield to critics for several crucial months, neither countering critics' arguments nor accepting their invitations to explore some compromise solution.

The rationale, of course, was that full attention must be focused on the economic program until the summer tax and budget action was complete. This determination to control its policy agenda has been one of the Reagan administration's more impressive features, and it certainly explains why the president and his White House congressional operation could not give the AWACS sale priority. But the key economic battleground was the House, and on the AWACS issue the House was hopeless for the administration—the sale would stand or fall in the Senate. It is hard to see how some forceful substantive lobbying of senators would have undercut the economic lobbying efforts on the other side of the Hill.

A more credible explanation for neglect is that no one the president trusted really understood either the issue or the broader politics of foreign policy. Haig, whose subsequent congressional testimony suggests that he understood both, remained on shaky probation. So until Reagan and his troika could be seriously engaged, lesser officials—national security assistant Richard Allen, Under Secretary of State James Buckley, Under Secretary of Defense Fred Iklé—could do little more than fight a holding action, when they were not caught up in interagency wrangling. Buckley, by most reports, was more effective on Capitol Hill than most others. But not until the legislative countdown began in September and the White House faced preliminary vote counts on the order of sixty-five senators opposed and twelve in favor did the president and his circle become deeply and personally engaged.

In the meantime, critics had much the best of it. The threat to Israel, political as well as military, was a necessary argument, and the American Israel Public Affairs Committee (AIPAC) was in the forefront of the opposition campaign. But in itself this was not sufficient. Broadening the critics' base and giving them greater credibility was concern about the compromise of American technology. The only arms sale to non-Arabs that had encountered major congressional resistance in previous years had been the sale of the AWACS to the shah's Iran, and his fall before any of the planes were delivered underscored the danger of advanced American weaponry's falling into unfriendly hands in an unstable region. Finally, there was a sense that we were being black-mailed by the Saudis, who had avidly sought the AWACS and then turned our ability to deliver into a "test" of U.S.-Saudi relations. On the strength of these arguments, anti-AWACS lobbyists got thirty-four Democratic and twenty Republican senators to sign a June 24 letter to President Reagan opposing the sale and urging that he not submit it. On September 17 thirty-two Democrats and eighteen Republicans joined in cosponsoring the Packwood resolution to disapprove the sale.

Priority was supposed to shift to the AWACS issue after Reagan's July triumphs, but over the next two months things worsened still further. In August everybody left town—Reagan and his full troika to California, legislators to their constituencies. Congress was notified informally that the sale proposal would be transmitted shortly, with the manner and timing adroitly set so as to offend neither the legislators, who were out of town, nor Israeli Prime Minister Menachem Begin, who was soon to visit. Reagan also decided, according to the *New York Times*, that Begin was to be told that the "strategic cooperation" Reagan was offering was conditional on Israeli acquiescence in the AWACS sale. But no one was assigned the job of telling him, and the message went undelivered until he had left Washington.[3]

That fiasco in dealing with Israel was followed by one with the Saudis. As Senate prospects dimmed and support grew for the proposal with which Senator John Glenn (Democrat, Ohio) became identified— U.S.-Saudi coownership and comanagement of the AWACS—national security assistant Richard Allen met with Senators Baker and Glenn and a Saudi representative to discuss a possible renegotiation of the terms. Haig, however, refused to have any "blankety-blank senators making foreign policy," though he was himself unable to win significant new concessions from the Saudis. Thus, when he opened formal administration testimony on October 1, he had nothing new to offer, and the administration had the worst possible situation: the Saudi government had been approached for concessions many senators thought reasonable and had stonewalled in response. An earlier exploration of other options, before the prestige of the administration and the Saudis was committed, might have proved successful; but now the administration had visibly failed, and the legislative countdown had begun.

Over eight months the Reagan administration thus dug itself a very deep hole on the AWACS sale, causing Senator Sam Nunn (Democrat, Georgia) to suggest that, if the vote were on the administration's handling

3. Leslie H. Gelb, "Foreign Policy System Criticized by U.S. Aides," *New York Times*, October 19, 1981.

of the matter, the AWACS sale would go down by about 97 to 3. In the ninth month the president led the way out of the hole, winning a dramatic 52 to 48 victory. The AWACS sale was "an issue he never made," one thrust on him by the ongoing government, bearing no clear relation to his personal priorities or electoral mandate. This made it harder for him to convey conviction about the substantive case; that he was nonetheless able to fight it and win was a testament to his determination and pragmatism in using the resources available.

In waging the final campaign, coordinated at the White House by chief of staff Baker, the administration had five potential means to win Senate backing. It could campaign for *public* support, as Reagan had done so effectively on budget and taxes. It could employ *payoffs* on side issues—rewards or threats of punishment—to influence fence-sitting senators. It could emphasize *policy,* winning converts to the substance of its case or making policy concessions to its critics. It could make the claim of *party* to those Republicans inclined to opposition. Finally, it could make the bipartisan plea for the *presidency* that had worked for Carter on Panama: Ronald Reagan's international effectiveness should not be crippled, because this would undercut U.S. influence in the world. It was the last two that proved most important.

Publicity. What is remarkable about the administration's public campaign is how little there was of it. Testimony was given in Senate hearings. The president made strong, intermittent comments to the press that cannot have been very helpful: it was "not the business of other nations to make American foreign policy"; "we will not permit Saudi Arabia to be an Iran"; senators who opposed the sale "are not doing their country a service." But there was no nationwide television address, not even a presidential speech, to put the AWACS issue in broader policy perspective. This omission was probably wise—a cogent, effective AWACS speech would have been hard to make, and the phone banks in the provinces might not have responded favorably.

Payoffs and Punishments. On any major foreign policy vote, the question of rewards and punishments on ancillary issues is always "in the air." An administration seeks, at a minimum, to convey two competing impressions: that the White House rewards its friends and punishes those who oppose it and that the president would not sully an issue of high policy by engaging in vote buying. The Reagan White House appears to have been effective at conveying both impressions. Nothing has yet come out publicly, however, to establish that anyone's vote on the AWACS was successfully "bought" or even "rented," although Senators Charles E. Grassley (Republican, Iowa) and Dennis DeConcini (Democrat, Arizona) reported what they thought were quid pro quo offers, and Senator Rudy Boschwitz (Republican, Minnesota) learned that a federal facility was being closed in Minnesota just after his negative vote in committee.

Policy. When it finally engaged the issue substantively, the administration was cogent in rebutting the critics' strongest arguments—in asserting that the AWACS sale was not a serious threat to Israel, that the risk to U.S. technology was limited and manageable. It was less effective in making a positive strategic case, in part because such a case rested on hopes for close U.S.-Saudi military cooperation that could not be explicitly stated. The administration had the greatest difficulty in establishing a clear Saudi commitment to a continuing U.S. role in AWACS operations. The royal government refused, for reasons of pride and regional standing, to play the American game that Panama had reluctantly played in 1977 and 1978—it refused to make concessions, real or symbolic, that senators could use politically to justify their conversion from skepticism to support.

This put the White House in a bind, for few senators were likely to switch without some policy rationale—few would wish to say, as did Iowa Republican Roger Jepsen, that "nothing much has changed but me." But adversity bred the major contribution of the AWACS issue to the instruments of executive-congressional relations: the *ever-changing presidential letter*. At the suggestion of Senator Nunn, endorsed and pressed by Senator John W. Warner (Republican, Virginia), Reagan agreed to send to the Senate majority leader a letter of unilateral U.S. assurances. The president encouraged senators he was wooing to propose draft language, which was incorporated as far as possible. Thus the document, retained in the White House, had ever-changing words if not substance. It was formally released and transmitted the day of the vote, after the White House had the necessary votes and too late for critics to attack it. And vulnerable to attack it certainly was, for one is hard pressed to find in the document a single important condition or assurance not previously presented by administration officials, beginning in early September. But it provided a convenient bridge or rationale for those switching from opposition to support.

Still, substantive bargaining—real or pretended—played a limited role in the victory, as evidenced by the fact that a number of those who did come to the president's side—most dramatically Senator William S. Cohen (Republican, Maine)—insisted that they still thought the sale a bad idea.

Party. In June twenty Republicans went on record against the sale. Only twelve opposed it in October, and at least two of them were said to have promised to switch if their votes were needed. One reason why the administration leaned on Republicans was that Democrats were moving the other way: the eleventh-hour opposition of Senator Robert C. Byrd (Democrat, West Virginia), the minority leader, underscored how much the AWACS sale was becoming a party issue, as only four of thirty-two northern Democrats voted in its favor. In any case, a number of Republicans who had signed the original Packwood letter stood out as obvious targets: Orrin G. Hatch of Utah, Alan Simpson of Wyoming, Slade Gorton of Washington, S. I. Hayakawa of California, Mark Andrews of North Dakota, Larry Pressler of South Dakota, and Grassley. Jepsen and Cohen were more surprising converts, particularly Jepsen in view of his early militant opposition. But to win them over was to perform what Mark Shields aptly labels "the most difficult of all" lobbying tasks: "to persuade any legislator to change positions on an issue publicly."[4]

Reagan persuaded nine Republicans and Senator Edward Zorinsky of Nebraska on the Democratic side to do this. Indispensable to this process, by all accounts, was Majority Leader Baker, who managed simultaneously to press his flock and to protect them, to search smoothly, constructively, yet relentlessly for ways that would enable enough of them to come around, and yet to insist all the while that it was not a partisan issue. Their particular stakes in Reagan's reputation and in their own capacity to control the Senate were stressed throughout; yet the majority leader seems also to have avoided burning bridges to those whom he could not persuade this time but might need another day.

Presidency. In the end Reagan's ultimate argument was the argument from weakness: you cannot afford to destroy me, your only president. More than once he was publicly quoted as pleading, "You're going to cut me off at the knees. I won't be effective in conducting foreign policy." He sounded strangely like his predecessor. Asked to explain how President Carter had won ratification of the Panama treaty three-and-a-half years before, aides said that, in the end, their most effective argument had been that Americans could not afford to have their president's international prestige demolished by a major foreign policy repudiation so early in his term. So it proved also with Ronald Reagan in October 1981. Herblock might see irony in this pitch coming from the militant critic of the Panama treaty and SALT II; but the pitch

4. Mark Shields, "Howard Baker's Hand," *Washington Post,* November 30, 1981.

worked. The peroration of Senator Alan Cranston (Democrat, California) on October 28 contained some exaggeration but much truth:

> We have heard Senator after Senator explain in great and persuasive detail why they believe the AWACS package is a bad mistake. Then we have heard the big "but." But, they say, despite the evils of the package, the President has made a decision and we must support the President; the President must conduct foreign policy; the Senate must support the Commander in Chief.[5]

And for those like Senator J. James Exon (Democrat, Nebraska), who denied that "any president must always be supported in foreign policy decisions," there was the related argument that "the president's commitment" had to prove decisive, since rejecting it would mean "our ability to follow through on a promise would be called into question." Thus, as Henry Kissinger had argued, it was a mistake to have agreed to the AWACS sale in the first place, but it would be a worse mistake to go back on the commitment once made.

These were, it should be emphasized, very valid circumstantial arguments. But the fact that the AWACS sale relied so heavily on them meant that the substantive case had lost in the American political arena. The White House–Senate team of Baker and Baker proved enormously effective. The president, in the final days, was by all accounts extraordinarily persuasive one on one, as he had been on economic policy several months before. But this time he was not triumphing, he was just surviving.

Foreign Aid: The Triumph of Pragmatism

It got far less publicity, but beginning early in the year and continuing through the AWACS fight and into December was the Reagan administration's most comprehensive foreign policy engagement with Congress —that over foreign aid legislation. On this issue, unlike the AWACS issue, it was subcabinet officials at the State Department, like Under Secretary Buckley and Assistant Secretary Richard Fairbanks, who carried the main lobbying burden, with indispensable reinforcement from the White House—and the president personally—at key points.

To many, Ronald Reagan seemed miscast as a champion of foreign aid, particularly in a year of budgetary stringency, but his administration saw budgetary and statutory changes in aid programs as critical to its foreign policy effectiveness. Specifically, it proposed

5. *Congressional Record*, October 28, 1981, p. S12450.

to reallocate funds from multilateral to bilateral programs and from development-oriented to politically targeted and military assistance, and it sought greater flexibility in the use of the funds. Yet as late as the Thanksgiving recess it seemed unlikely that any aid legislation would be enacted in 1981. Separate authorizing and appropriating bills had passed the Senate, but neither had reached the floor of the House of Representatives, where support was uncertain. Even if approved there, each bill would need to go to conference to resolve House-Senate differences and then return to each body for endorsement before Congress adjourned for Christmas.

What was the new administration seeking? The Carter FY 1982 aid budget had proposed a substantial rise over 1981 in development programs and a modest increase in military and politically targeted funds: the Economic Support Fund (ESF), military aid, and arms sales credits. The Reagan budget of March reversed this emphasis, and early action in the authorization and appropriations committees generally sustained this reversal, particularly in the Senate. The administration got a cooler reception for its main proposal for flexibility: that contingency money not allocated to a specific country be added to the ESF and to authorizations and appropriations for military aid. Its original proposal was for $250 million and $100 million, respectively: the House Foreign Affairs Committee recommended $100 million and $25 million, and the Senate Foreign Relations Committee deleted all this money from its bill, "primarily for budgetary reasons." The two appropriations subcommittees included reduced amounts in their bills.

Finally, the administration sought repeal or relaxation of country-specific restrictions barring covert aid to factions in Angola (the Clark amendment), military aid to Argentina, and aid to Pakistan unless it gave explicit assurances of nuclear nonproliferation (the Symington amendment). Here only the two authorizing committees were involved. On the Clark amendment, the House Foreign Affairs Committee said no, but the administration won conditional repeal in the Senate Foreign Relations Committee. On Argentina both committees agreed to repeal subject to presidential reporting on progress in human rights. On Pakistan the House committee voted no pending information on the details of the proposed country aid program and the administration's broader national security policy. The Senate committee kept the language of the Symington amendment but allowed it to be waived for Pakistan and also required reports on the detailed program and "the President's current nonproliferation policy."[6]

6. Quotations are from the House and Senate committee reports.

The authorizing committees did their work expeditiously, reporting out separate House and Senate bills in May just six weeks after transmission of the administration's draft proposal. But rather than being moved expeditiously to the floor, the bills were held back as the president's economic program dominated the congressional agenda. After the White House signaled in the summer that the foreign aid bill had high priority with the president, the full Senate gave it substantial floor time: five days in September and October. The process was much smoother than in past years. Percy, the floor manager, worked out most of the issues under contention with State Department representatives, the Senate leadership, and committee colleagues. The administration won several victories: full repeal of the Clark amendment, restoration of aid contingency money (after Reagan reduced the amounts requested as part of his September budget cuts), and an unsolicited but welcome relaxation of the ban on aid to Chile, which was so carefully crafted it won the support of both Edward Kennedy and Jesse Helms.

Balanced against these gains for the administration was the addition of unwanted new constraints on aid to El Salvador. Adopting language similar to that approved by the House Foreign Affairs Committee in May, the full Senate voted to condition aid on a presidential certification, to be made every six months, of progress by the government of El Salvador toward several related goals: safeguarding human rights; controlling the armed forces to end "indiscriminate torture and murder"; "implementing economic and political reforms, including the land reform program"; holding free elections; and demonstrating willingness to negotiate a political resolution of the conflict. An administration-backed effort by Senator Richard Lugar (Republican, Indiana) to change these conditions to nonbinding congressional preferences lost by 47 to 51. On this Percy opposed the administration, as he had not on other major floor issues, and carried a majority of Foreign Relations Committee Republicans with him. The full Senate also enacted an absolute prohibition against aid to any state without nuclear weapons that exploded a nuclear device. The administration reluctantly endorsed the prohibition in order to supplant a Glenn amendment that singled out India and Pakistan.

The final vote on October 22 signaled a shift in party responsibility. For the first time in recent memory, foreign aid got more Republican (23 to 16) than Democratic (17 to 17) support, although it was generally the liberals in both parties who voted in its favor. And when the Senate broke precedent a month later by taking up its own aid appropriations bill rather than waiting for the House, the bill was passed in one day with broad (57 to 33) bipartisan backing.

79

If the Senate was moving forward, however, the House was standing still. Mustering a foreign aid majority was expected to prove particularly difficult in a year when the domestic budget was being squeezed, and Clement Zablocki (Democrat, Wisconsin), chairman of the Foreign Affairs Committee, made it known that he was unwilling to have the Democrats bear the brunt of the political burden as in past years, when their votes for foreign aid had been eagerly exploited by Republican challengers. This year Zablocki wanted bipartisan support, and he would not move for floor consideration unless the White House could supply him with a list of 125 Republicans committed to vote yes.

His concerns were amply vindicated on September 17 when only forty Republicans supported the FY 1982 State Department authorization bill, which was rejected 165 to 226. There were several apparent causes, including confusion about the administration's position and the fact that the amounts in the bill were slightly higher than in the revised Reagan budget. But one reason was, as senior Republican Edward Derwinski of Illinois explained, "A lot of the freshmen thought they were voting on foreign aid." Once this matter was clarified and the numbers were reduced to Reagan-certified levels, the House Republican leadership got fully behind the State Department bill. It then passed comfortably on October 29 by 317 to 58, with 145 Republicans in favor. The aid authorization still languished, however, as Zablocki awaited his list.

Aid appropriations were caught in a separate but related House tangle. The basic subcommittee fight was between development advocates, such as Democrats Matthew McHugh of New York and David Obey of Wisconsin, and backers of military and politically targeted programs, led by Republican Jack Kemp of New York. The appropriations bill also included the politically vulnerable funds for the International Development Agency (IDA)—the "soft loan window" of the World Bank—which the Carter administration had pledged and its successor was reluctantly supporting, albeit in reduced annual amounts.

Supporters of the IDA had managed a minor miracle by getting their authorization bill, which no one thought would win an up-or-down House vote, attached to the omnibus reconciliation bill of July. Reagan had clinched this arrangement by making phone calls to IDA critics Kemp and Bill Young (Republican, Florida), after other budget issues he cared about were resolved. To get money appropriated for the IDA, Democrats led by McHugh proposed a bipartisan bargain: they would back the administration's political and military aid proposals in exchange for floor backing by Kemp and Young of the full bill, including the IDA. Kemp and Young agreed not to fight the bill on the floor, but they wanted leeway on IDA cuts. The Democrats said "no deal": the bill reported by the House Appropriations Committee contained less than the administration wanted in political-military money and was vulnerable to floor assault.

With the House Foreign Operations Subcommittee thus unable to promise unity on the floor, prospects for enactment of a separate aid appropriations bill appeared increasingly dim. So the administration lent its encouragement to a strategy pressed by Senate Appropriations Subcommittee Chairman Robert Kasten (Republican, Wisconsin), to fund aid by continuing resolution as in the past two years, but at levels that reflected Reagan's policy priorities. This would make the aid appropriations bill unnecessary, although an authorization act would still of course be required. Spurning the usual procedure of waiting for the House, the Senate committee reported out its own aid money bill and brought it to the floor. Going beyond what was apparently the original plan, to take the bill to the brink of passage (the third reading) and stop, the Senate passed the bill in mid-November. The next day Kasten put forward a technical amendment that got the bill's money figures inserted into the comprehensive continuing resolution required to keep the government functioning after November 20. The Senate could thus take its numbers directly to conference.

Chairman Clarence Long (Democrat, Maryland) of the House Foreign Operations Subcommittee was outraged at this usurpation of his own, and the House's, prerogatives. In alliance with the House Democratic leadership, he was able to thwart Kasten's strategy by insisting on continuing resolution figures for aid much lower than the administration could accept. And when the president pressed to increase them, Democrats could not resist the political opportunity. Was it really true, one after another of them asked rhetorically on the House floor, that the same president who had told the public he was vetoing the bill because it spent too much had actually been pressing the conferees to add "more for foreign aid for foreign countries," at the expense of domestic programs?

In fighting Kasten, however, Long ended by promoting the goal they both favored—getting a real aid appropriations bill enacted. As Congress recessed for Thanksgiving, it faced the task of passing another continuing resolution by December 15. But it was clear that the politics of the continuing resolution process would generate aid numbers too low to be acceptable to the administration—they simply could not be raised in the same bill that was squeezing domestic programs. So the administration had to undertake the arduous task of getting two aid bills through the House in December—and then to conference and final approval in both bodies—at the same time that the larger funding dispute was being resolved.

Zablocki changed his position modestly—instead of insisting on a list of Republican names, he would move the authorizing bill to the floor to give the Republicans the opportunity to provide decisive support. Speaker O'Neill reinforced this by saying that Democrats would provide their share of aid votes if Reagan could produce his. Democrats on the Appropriations Committee indicated that they would support the committee bill on the floor as long as it was not significantly altered; if conservatives slashed development money or attached restrictions like those proposed by Young on the use of funds by international organizations, then the responsibility was all theirs. So the administration, out of necessity, backed the bills as reported by committees that were substantially more liberal than either the House as a whole or the Reagan administration, and it took on the long-proposed task of mobilizing the needed Republican support.

When the bills reached the floor, Republican-sponsored amendments were few, and successful ones even fewer. Kemp emerged as a vocal and effective advocate of aid. Although he did win a floor amendment reducing IDA funds by $125 million, its main effect was to block another amendment cutting those funds by $330 million. In the authorization debate, Derwinski took the floor to explain that "in the interest of expediting this bill" he was withholding his proposal to repeal the Clark amendment.

The House passed the aid authorization by 222 to 184 on Wednesday, December 9, and the appropriations bill by 199 to 166 two days later. Both were rushed to conference to reconcile Senate-House differences and achieve final bills before the adjournment planned for mid-month. White House pressure continued, as did Reagan's personal involvement, and the fact that any contested issue would make enactment in December impossible further increased the leverage of Democrats, whose opposition to a conference report could prove fatal. Thus the administration sustained several significant losses in conference.

It had won repeal of the Clark amendment in the Senate and might have prevailed on this point in conference, but that might have lost enough Democrats in the House to block final passage. So, after Reagan called Zablocki and heard his bleak prognosis, the administration decided to back off, and it was Helms who made the motion to recede. This concession eased the way, however, for agreement on lifting the bans on arms sales to Argentina and Chile.

The final bill did give the president the urgently sought right to waive for Pakistan the ban on aid to countries receiving nuclear enrichment technology outside international safeguards. It also gave Congress a new right to veto a related presidential waiver by concurrent resolution. The administration had been fighting such a veto, and its Senate allies thought that the conference agreement did not include one, but Senator John Glenn (Democrat, Ohio), Representative Stephen Solarz (Democrat, New York), and Representative Jonathan B. Bingham (Democrat, New York) argued that it did, and the administration went along to avoid spending the time it would take to fight it and the risk to final passage.

On the appropriations side, the administration also made concessions to liberals because of the limited size and the fragility of the House support coalition. Rather than splitting the difference in money figures, the conference provided all of the higher House amount for development assistance through the Agency for International Development (AID) and almost all of the higher House figure for the IDA. On military aid, for which the Senate had provided $1.096 billion and the House $924 million, the conference agreed on $965 million. Contingency money was essentially eliminated. And because of complications in the congressional budget process, the conferees dropped $250 million that had been provided in "off budget" money for a special defense acquisition fund, which the administration had sought to allow the Defense Department to make advance purchases of weapons frequently sold abroad.

Having made these concessions, the administration was able to win quick House adoption of the two conference reports on Wednesday, December 16, approximately ten hours before its adjournment sine die.

Press accounts have tended to exaggerate the number of Republicans who switched to support of aid on final passage. Republicans had split 58 to 82 against the authorization bill in June 1980; on the three votes in December 1981 they were divided 97 to 86 (authorization), 84 to 87 (appropriations), and 91 to 93 (appropriations conference report). Of the seventy-five current Republican members who voted no in 1980, only nineteen voted yes on two or more of the 1981 bills, and they were partially offset by the six Republicans who shifted the other way. Thus the net swing was thirteen. But certain key Republicans who voted no—like Trent Lott of Mississippi and Bill Young—cooperated in expediting the bills. It was left to the fringe Republican John Ashbrook of Ohio to offer the inevitable amendment barring "indirect" aid to Cuba, Vietnam, etc.; this amendment (though cosponsored by Kemp) was not pushed to a recorded vote. Still, it was northern Democrats who provided the core support for aid, although their 2 to 1 margin in favor was less than in previous years. The failure of Republicans to vote comparably enabled the Democrats, by threatening withdrawal of support, to press priorities that up-or-down floor votes would not normally have sustained. The fact that Obey did vote no signaled that this was not an idle threat.

Some Concluding Thoughts

How should an administration go about building a congressional base for foreign policy? In practice, its initial course will depend on what it seeks to accomplish substantively. If it opts for maximum change, for carrying out a sweeping mandate real or presumed, it will necessarily concentrate on generating and maintaining momentum, on mobilizing advocates on its side of the domestic divide to do battle with its adversaries. Such a maximalist approach will please its own ideologues, but simultaneously nourish the ideologues in opposition. It is also likely to become highly partisan, since it gains force from electoral victory and repudiation of the party recently displaced. Finally, as argued by Senator John Tower (Republican, Texas) in *Foreign Affairs,* if the policy change sought is in the direction of worldwide political-military activism, the administration will need to minimize congressional involvement in policy detail, even perhaps to seek repeal of most of the statutory constraints that Congress imposed in the 1970s.[7] At a minimum, it will probably involve repeated confrontation with the responsible congressional committees.

Alternatively, a new administration might move more cautiously, changing policy selectively and carefully, consulting widely, and seeking broad support. Such a moderate approach might seek to minimize the ideological content of policy and build a centrist political coalition that would share the political burden of diverting resources to support foreign and national security policy at a time of domestic pain. This approach would generate some discontent within the administration's camp: true believers would need to be reined in, party adversaries ceded virtues they were denied in the election campaign. And it would deny the administration the political appeal that comes, at least initially, from a new beginning. As argued by Senator Percy in *Foreign Policy,* however, the result might just be the sort of durable bipartisan coalition of internationalists that sustained American world engagement in the first two postwar decades,[8] and it could be based, in the main, on cooperation with established congressional power centers.

7. John Tower, "Congress versus the President," *Foreign Affairs* (Winter 1981/82), pp. 229-46.
8. Charles Percy, "The Partisan Gap," *Foreign Policy* (Winter 1981-82), pp. 3-15.

No administration opts purely for one course or the other, but the Reagan regime came to power leaning strongly in the maximalist direction, and not just on foreign policy. On economic policy the White House proposed major changes in course, confronted its adversaries, and quickly emerged triumphant. So it did also on defense, though to a lesser degree, since the Carter administration had also been pushing rapid military expansion in its final years. On foreign policy, however, the maximalist approach brought mostly trouble. Pressing for ideological victory proved workable when the nominee was a Haig but disastrous when he was a Lefever and irrelevant when he was a Crocker or Rashish. By drawing the line in El Salvador and seeming to renounce concern for human rights, the administration promptly gave new life to liberal causes that seemed dead in late 1980: no more Vietnams, America as a beacon of liberty. By the fall of 1981, Reagan's rhetoric and perceived policies had strengthened the antinuclear movement in Europe and served as midwife to a sister movement at home, the first grass-roots stirring for arms control that the United States had seen in years. These reactions pushed policy back toward the center: the spotlight was taken from El Salvador; Elliott Abrams, assistant secretary of state for human rights and humanitarian affairs, developed a more positive human rights approach; and Ronald Reagan embraced the "zero solution" in Europe.

The administration was also driven toward a more moderate approach by the need to win on the AWACS sale and aid. The enactment of foreign assistance required compromise with liberal Democrats; avoiding humiliation on the arms sale required the president to play the traditional "above politics" role of national foreign policy leader. And Percy, his difficult personality notwithstanding, had proved that his bipartisan approach could deliver results for the administration—and, on occasion, against it. Republicans were still summoned to support their president, which they did adequately in the House on aid and overwhelmingly in the Senate on the dramatic AWACS test. But the call was not so much to vindicate their party platform as to share the burdens of exercising power, of governing the nation. This was the sort of appeal that could win Republicans without losing Democrats. And it was consistent with the president's above-party role as guardian of the national interest, from which he can draw decisive political power on international issues, as the AWACS struggle attests.

Will the shift toward moderation endure? Specific compromises on aid were forced by the particular legislative context, above all the excruciating time squeeze. In 1982 one would expect the Reagan administration to seek substantial further shifts in the aid balance between development and political-military funds and to press again for repeal of constraints like the Clark amendment.

Will it prove successful? One could argue that the maximalist approach would have done much better in 1981 had the White House not put foreign policy on the back burner for most of the year and had the secretary of state not been diverted by hand-to-hand combat with the counselor to the president and the secretary of defense. But there are also some hard facts of life in the politics of foreign policy that seem to limit what this approach can achieve.

First, as already stressed, this approach energizes an administration's ideological adversaries and cedes them some high political ground, as Reagan originally did on human rights, arms sales, and arms control. This would not be crucial if foreign policy were inherently popular and politically rewarding. After all, during the defense appropriations debate in the Senate the Reagan program galvanized Democrats into putting forward amendment after amendment, proposing to shift funds from the B-1 and other ventures prized by the administration to different defense uses. They lost on all of them and then voted overwhelmingly for final passage. But preparedness is popular; foreign policy, far less expensive and arguably more cost effective in many cases, is not. Hence the second fact of life: American foreign policy in today's world is simply not attractive enough as a political enterprise to be sustained by Congress if an administration alienates half the natural constituency of internationalism. This conclusion is independent of whether the administration comes to be viewed as too "soft" or too "hard."

Thus the 1981 experience with aid provides an apt metaphor. It is not easy to get Jack Kemp, Clarence Long, and liberals like Matt McHugh into the same policy boat. But unless we can, the boat is unlikely to stay afloat for very long.

Two final lessons suggest themselves from this review of Reagan, Congress, and foreign policy:

An administration must try to think whole: to anticipate the impact of congressional politics on foreign policy, and vice versa. To those who lived through the congressional battles of the Carter years—Panama, Middle East arms sales—how the AWACS issue would unfold was predictable. To sustain a counterintuitive policy action with domestic politics skewed against it, the administration would have to make it a major political drama, a test of presidential credibility. Both opponents and would-be supporters would shine a critical spotlight on Saudi Arabia, the former to discredit it as a fit partner, the latter to extract concessions that would help justify (and rationalize) their support. The president and his team would need to devote major personal time to this issue, which would further tie their prestige to its outcome. The willingness to invest this political capital was bound to shake the Israelis, notwithstanding that it was Israel's U.S. supporters who made the investment necessary. The public furor was also likely to drive the Saudis to demonstrate their continued independence. Was it worth it? My judgment is that it was not, that the AWACS sale was avoidable and should have been avoided. The more telling point is that no one who favored plunging ahead in the early spring had, it appears, the slightest awareness of these predictable consequences. No one put policy and politics together. Thus the AWACS issue illustrates the ease with which a new administration can carelessly squander valuable assets—its reputation for competence, the president's time and prestige—by leaping before it looks.

Good executive branch policy making makes for congressional effectiveness, and vice versa. Reagan's foreign policy system in general performed poorly on the AWACS issue. By March the military arm had gone ahead of the diplomatic-political arm, making commitments to Saudi Arabia without assessing their costs or exploring alternatives like comanagement. In September disorganization led to mishandling of the Begin summit and to feuding between Haig and Allen over whether Saudi concessions should be sought and who should do the seeking. There was throughout no serious linkage of the fact and timing of the Saudi AWACS sale to a broader policy strategy for the region. In fact, the sale seemed to undercut the administration's declared strategy by raising tensions between two of the three countries that were essential to the policy of anti-Soviet "strategic consensus."

Nor was the AWACS sale the only issue on which executive disarray brought the Reagan administration trouble in Congress—this was evident in the nomination fights of the spring as well. Congress always listens more to an administration that seems to know what it is doing and to officials who have credible presidential backing.

The AWACS sale was ultimately saved by top White House political-congressional operators, including the president, but they started out by making things worse. They trusted Weinberger, who knew little, over Haig, who knew much more. The president showed no awareness of how far his personal credibility was being invested. And in banning substantive lobbying on the AWACS question until the summer budget and tax battles were completed, the senior White House staff dug the president's hole deeper. Once the clock was running, however, they did much better, aided by their Senate allies Percy, Tower, and above all the majority leader, Howard Baker.

A better coordinated foreign policy operation in the executive branch would almost certainly broaden the administration's congressional effectiveness, just as it would improve its reputation at home and abroad. The designation of William Clark as national security assistant seems a step in the right direction, given his old ties to Reagan and the mutual confidence he and Haig established at the State Department. But the core problem remains the tenuous relation between Reagan and Haig, which serves to weaken both men. Unless Reagan replaces Haig or finds a way to work effectively with him—or takes day-to-day control of foreign policy himself, an unlikely event—continued disarray is likely.

Assessing Reagan's First Year

Norman J. Ornstein

As 1981 drew to a close, Senate Majority Leader Howard Baker summed up the year in Congress by saying, "Men and women will disagree on the policies adopted by this Congress and this administration, but almost no one, I think, will dispute the proposition that this Congress has made more fundamental changes in the public policy of this nation than any Congress in decades."

Even making allowances for partisan hyperbole, few would dispute the contention that the first session of the Ninety-seventh Congress was remarkable. A new president decisively focused public and congressional attention on one issue, economic recovery; induced virtually all political actors to accept his basic premises on this issue (that is, the need for domestic budget cuts, defense increases, and tax cuts to improve capital formation and investment); and reduced the issue to three beautifully timed blockbuster keynotes, all well defined and highly publicized, and all smashing victories for the president. All this occurred before August 1981; after that the president's work would be more difficult. Nonetheless, a total assessment of Reagan's first year with Congress must be positive.

President Reagan's first year (and the first session of the Ninety-seventh Congress) contrasts with the first year of President Carter and the Ninety-fifth Congress. At the end of 1977, Jimmy Carter's standing with the American people was reasonably strong (indeed, it was slightly higher than Reagan's in a comparable Gallup poll in 1981!), but no congressional leader summed up the first session of the Ninety-fifth Congress with effusive praise or dramatic assertions of accomplishments. Carter did not focus public and congressional attention on a key issue. He failed to forge a consensus on the basics if not the details, and he was not persuasive or strong enough to win dramatically over congressional opponents.

Carter lacked a focal point in the first year of his presidency. The closest he came to an overall issue comparable to Reagan's economic

89

plan was in his energy policy. In mid-April 1977 Carter proposed a comprehensive energy plan, more than two months after he had delivered a televised "fireside chat" on energy conservation. With strong assistance from House Speaker Thomas (Tip) O'Neill and the help of an innovative House procedure that set up an unusual ad hoc energy committee, the basics of the Carter plan were passed by the House of Representatives in August by a vote of 244 to 177. This was a big victory for Carter. The plan soon faltered, however, on a filibuster in the Senate. News of the ongoing major problems of the Carter energy plan in the Senate competed with news concerning Bert Lance's problem through September and October. Most news stories on the energy plan suggested that the Senate was "gutting" the Carter proposal. In October the Senate finally passed a watered-down version of the plan, minus energy taxes, but the plan then stalled in a conference committee. After three weeks of stalemate, Carter dramatically canceled a four-continent foreign tour and gave a nationally televised address on his energy program to rally public support. When Congress adjourned six weeks later on December 15, 1977, however, the energy conferees were still deadlocked. Frustration and disappointment prevailed.

Although this paper is about Ronald Reagan, comparisons with Carter's first year are essential if we are to understand what Reagan did and did not accomplish, and why. They also help us, at the next stage, to sort out what might occur with Reagan and the Congress in 1982.

Ronald Reagan and Jimmy Carter are quite different individuals—with different styles, abilities, and philosophies. Clearly, this is a major reason for differences in perception, performance, and results in 1977 and in 1981. Circumstances also matter, and Reagan had a series of initial advantages (some, to be sure, which he himself caused or shaped) which eased the path for his successes.

Initial Reagan Advantages

Ronald Reagan came to Washington with a number of distinct advantages, including the results, common interpretation, and historical context of the 1980 election, the nature of public sentiment at the time, and the experiences of his predecessor. Reagan's own skill and determination heightened these advantages. Nonetheless, it is still important to catalog the positive and negative elements of the political environment that the new president encountered.

The Election. The election was an important plus for Reagan in several respects. First, he won convincingly. There was no question of either his legitimacy or his political pulling power. Unlike his predecessor, Reagan did not begin with a big lead after the party conventions, only to see it dwindle substantially at the end. Instead, support for Reagan grew steadily, and he outdrew a sizable number of Republican legislators in their own districts and states.

Carter, in contrast, carried only 220 of 435 congressional districts —and did better than only twenty-two Democratic congressmen on their own home turf. Although Carter was greeted with the wave of affection and respect we traditionally accord our new presidents, there was no strong sense of awe or respect for his political or electoral skills. He limped to victory, whereas Reagan waltzed.

Second, the 1980 election provided the new president with perhaps the *single most important* element in the subsequent success of Reagan's policies—a Republican Senate. The Republican Senate gave the president much more leverage over the political agenda and the timing of events than he ever would have possessed on his own. It was the Senate that adapted and applied the technique of early omnibus reconciliation to the Reagan budget requests; it was the Senate that acted first on the initial budget resolution. In both cases, the House of Representatives was forced to act before it wanted to act, in a climate distinctly favorable to the president. In both cases, the history and tradition of the House acting first on money matters was ignored. A Democratic Senate, with Democratic committee chairmen, would not have behaved in this fashion.

The Republican majority in the Senate also gave the president breathing room and allowed him to conserve and concentrate his political resources. A cohesive Senate majority party dedicated to the president's main goals could be safely ignored in the battle of persuasion, and counted on to go along with the White House. All the firepower could be concentrated on the recalcitrant House. The White House would not have considered a Senate with a Democratic majority as reliable—even if there were a conservative majority. The lobbying efforts of the president and his staff would have been more diverted, more diffused.

In addition, the election of a Republican Senate altered entirely the broader interpretations given by politicians and pundits alike to the 1980 election. Reagan plus the Republican Senate equaled a realignment in the making. Reagan without the Republican Senate would have represented a personal defeat for Jimmy Carter, not for the Democratic party. To substantiate this claim, we need only go back eight years, to 1972, when the Republicans experienced an even greater landslide victory for the White House. Richard Nixon in 1972 outdid Ronald Reagan in 1980 by ten full percentage points in the popular vote and by 31 electoral votes. But Nixon's election was not accompanied by big Republican victories elsewhere; in fact, the Republicans actually lost seats in the Senate. When Nixon was reinaugurated on January 20, 1973, he continued to face confident and combative Democratic majorities in both houses of Congress, both complacent in their continued long-term success at the polls. Americans did not reject Democrats in 1972—they rejected *George McGovern* for president.

Had Reagan's election been accompanied by continued Democratic control of the Senate, 1980 would have been interpreted as a rejection of Carter. Democrats in the House and Senate for the twenty-seventh consecutive year would have greeted the new president and his proposals positively but without enthusiasm. Democrats would have been much less dizzy and demoralized than they turned out to be. The entire political climate would have been quite different.

Finally, Republican control of the Senate occurred for the first time in the political lives of nearly all members of Congress. For all but two Republican senators and two Republican House members, life in Congress before 1981 had meant perpetual minority status. A minority party that moves into the majority after a long period wandering in the desert exhibits early and striking party cohesion. Had the Republicans moved into majority status in Congress two or four years before Reagan's election, or had majority status been less novel to them, they probably would have displayed less party unity on key votes in 1981.

In contrast, Carter entered the White House accompanied by healthy Democratic majorities in both houses of Congress, as had been the case for the previous twenty-two years. Carter did not contribute either to the existence of his party's congressional majority or to its size (the 2-to-1 party edge in the House and the 62-to-38 margin in the Senate had been forged in 1974). Although new Democratic party leaders were selected in the House and Senate after the 1976 election, they were political veterans who had seen presidents come and go with little effect on themselves or the majority. The new leaders in fact had been in the majority for their entire congressional careers. Their own success was independent of presidential performance and behavior. Similarly, for their rank-and-file colleagues, success and the advantages of majority status had often been achieved and maintained without the need of party or president—and sometimes in spite of the party's presidential candidate.

Public sentiment also worked to Reagan's advantage. William Schneider has demonstrated convincingly in *The American Elections of 1980* that the presidential election was a referendum on the Carter administration—and the public voted convincingly for change.[1] The strong public desire for change gave President Reagan's bold plan a major boost, both initially and at various steps along the way in 1981. Schneider also shows a public with much stronger views about giving the new president an opportunity to make changes than about implementing any specific programs—and a public united behind the belief that the overriding problem facing America was the economy and, in particular, inflation.

Carter, in contrast, faced a public that was not concerned over a clear and overriding issue. Inflation, energy, unemployment, crime, foreign affairs—all had their place in the pantheon of public concerns. The public was also deeply divided over what to do about these problems. In other words, there was no consensus on the solutions to major national problems, or on the nature of the problems themselves. Carter made the White House and the presidency more plebeian and less mystifying, sold the presidential yacht, and tried to remove any sense of awe and majesty from the Oval Office. Though refreshing at first, by 1980 this approach had become annoying.

Reagan benefited from the obvious contrasts with Carter in style and behavior and learned from his predecessor's mistakes. With public and journalistic approval, Reagan moved to restore formality and glory to the White House. In the process, he made visits to 1600 Pennsylvania Avenue and presidential cuff links rewards to be coveted by members of Congress.

Carter had acquired a reputation of ineptitude and callousness in dealing with Congress. He started out on the wrong foot before the election, when calls from congressmen went unanswered. Mindful of Carter's experience, Reagan began in November, long before his inauguration, to build a strong reputation in the Washington community for political savvy and sensitivity in relationships with members of Congress. He hired two widely respected professional Congress hands, Bill Timmons and Tom Korologos, to manage his transition, and he chose another well-respected and experienced professional, Max Friedersdorf, to run his White House congressional liaison operation. He paid numerous well-timed and well-received visits to Capitol Hill, stroking Democrats and Republicans alike. Carter had been panned in January 1977 for allegedly denying Speaker O'Neill tickets to the inauguration; Reagan gave the Democratic Speaker a bountiful supply—and made sure everybody knew about it. Few of these steps were extraordinary. They were in stark contrast to steps taken by Carter, however, and Reagan used them forcefully and deliberately to

1. William Schneider, "The November 4 Vote for President: What Did It Mean?" in *The American Elections of 1980,* Austin Ranney, ed. (Washington, D.C.: American Enterprise Institute, 1981), pp. 212-62.

enhance his early reputation and to create from the beginning a more favorable climate for his program in Congress.

Reagan also benefited from Carter's early policy actions and experiences. Carter had been determined to "hit the ground running" in the first half of 1977. He sent a massive and impressive collection of complex legislative proposals to Capitol Hill, including a major tax cut package, a substantial budget revision, executive reorganization authority, election law reforms, a new Department of Energy, an anti-inflation package, food stamp policy revision, hospital cost containment, an ethics-in-government bill, social security reform, labor law reform, and welfare reform, not to mention the sweeping energy proposals discussed earlier. Except in a pallid way for the energy plan, however, there were no clear presidential priorities among these proposals—all were hyperbolically deemed crucial by Carter. A large number of the proposals were referred at practically the same time to the House Ways and Means Committee, where a kind of "gridlock" resulted. Few of the proposals went anywhere. Some—including the $50 rebate as part of the tax cut—were later withdrawn, abruptly and without notice, by the president. The overall result was that little was accomplished, Congress was overloaded, and the public was confused and distracted. Presidential attention and resources were diverted and fragmented. Opportunities that had existed early in the administration, when Carter's popularity and reputation were at a high point, were frittered away.

In 1981, Reagan, too, "hit the ground running." Unlike Carter, however, Reagan was wise enough to concentrate his attention, staff, and resources on the one overarching priority, reviving the national economy, and skillful enough to use every bit of his early leverage to put the basics of his plan in place. Reagan also was sensitive to the perils of sudden policy reversals, which so often characterized Carter's policy making and alienated allies of the administration.

Moreover, Carter's experience in the White House sensitized Reagan to the impact of political timing. Many times during his presidency, Carter tried to rally support for a position without considering what action might follow his appeal and when. He rarely seemed to link his public appeals for action to the political environment, or to recognize how he would be perceived if he concentrated his resources, prestige, and determination, blew the trumpet, yelled "Charge!" and . . . nothing.

The chief example of this is, once again, the energy package. As we recall, Carter angrily canceled his foreign tour on November 7, made a dramatic appeal for his energy plan over national television on November 8—and then, along with the rest of the country (which had become attentive after the Carter speech) watched helplessly as nothing happened. The conferees remained deadlocked for months thereafter.

In contrast, Reagan carefully marshaled his television appearances to promote his policies. Each was dramatic, and each was followed only a short time later by a key congressional vote. There was a risk involved, to be sure, but the president used these television appearances to maximize his leverage and enhance his reputation. The chances for success after each public appeal were enhanced, too, by a sophisticated and hard-nosed grass-roots campaign in the districts of wavering congressmen, aimed at generating pressure from campaign contributors and significant citizens, as well as common constituents. Reagan did not naively overrely on a spontaneous response.

The First Year's Performance

Early in his administration, Reagan established a positive image, which he reinforced often, an image that the press frequently made reference to when describing or outlining his presidency. Reagan came to be described as a man who was comfortable with the trappings of the highest office in the land, aware of the ins and outs of political power in Washington, surrounded by competent professionals, filled with humor, but tough as nails on matters of principle and policy. The positive image was reinforced with each stunning policy success. By skillfully orchestrating events, reinforcing this image, and narrowing the concentration of his efforts, Reagan made all political eyes focus on the big battles over budgets and tax cuts. Defeat on the issues of infant formula, wilderness areas, or the Lefever nomination, setbacks on aid to El Salvador and on social security, and dithering on clean air or the superfund were downplayed and discounted.

This is not to suggest that this portrayal reflected an unbalanced distortion of reality. Still, it is quite clear that the first year provided Reagan with numerous problems, gaffes, and minuses mixed in with the plusses. The Carter presidency's first year also had successes mixed with failures—but given his early image, the setbacks and gaffes were underscored, while the positive elements were downplayed and discounted.

During the furious maneuvering before the tax cut vote, the *Washington Post* ran a front-page story on the Reagan lobbying effort, cataloging the array of techniques the White House team was using to corral the recalcitrants. Only toward the end of the story, buried on a back page, was mention made of some small mistakes that had become apparent: a letter from liaison chief Max Friedersdorf to southern Democratic congressman Beryl Anthony of Arkansas had been mistakenly addressed to Rep. Anthony Beryl. Thus the importance of the positive image Reagan had built early for himself—how differently such a news item would have been reported had the president been Jimmy Carter and the liaison chief Frank Moore!

Clearly, as Stephen Wayne's paper demonstrates, there were *real* differences between the Moore shop and the Friedersdorf operation (not to mention the different outcomes in Congress) that justified different coverage in the press. After a disastrous start, the Carter congressional liaison operation pulled itself together before the end of the first year, but it never managed to recover from or erase its weak early image. The early image is a key factor in judging presidential performance. Today, however, one year into the Reagan administration, we can more coolly assess the successes and failures of Reagan's first year.

Setting the budget aside for the moment, we can see one clear Reagan coup, one serious gaffe, and two policy areas of ongoing difficulty and contention. The coup was the nomination of Sandra Day O'Connor as the first woman justice on the Supreme Court. In one stroke, President Reagan flabbergasted his critics on the left, disarmed his critics on the right, and broadened his political base in the middle. In the process, he diverted attention from other politically costly battles over unfortunate nominations to the Departments of State, Health and Human Services, and Defense.

The gaffe concerned cutbacks in social security. It would be hard to imagine the administration handling the issue any worse than it did. The president spurned an early opportunity to cooperate on a solution with House Democrats through the Pickle Social Security subcommittee and quashed an early plea by Senate Budget Committee Chairman Pete Domenici to give Senate Republicans an opening to grapple with social security increases. Then, without warning, the volatile administration plan was released in May. It met with little but scorn. A key political issue became a Republican albatross. Even though it would have been difficult under any circumstances for President Reagan to deal with social security without political damage, the impact of the administration's plan was much worse than it had to be. Despite Reagan's efforts to downplay the issue, it will reverberate through 1982.

The two broader subjects of contention are the environment and foreign policy. The Ninety-seventh Congress, though more conservative than its predecessors, is not intent on erasing all environmental edicts. The concern of congressmen for the environment is reflected strongly in public opinion polls, giving environmentalist legislators still more resolve to defend their position. The House Interior and Insular Affairs Committee clashed repeatedly in 1981 with Interior Secretary James G. Watt over water policy and wilderness areas, vetoing at one point Watt's proposed mineral leasing in Montana's Bob Marshall Wilderness Area. Congress as a whole rejected the Watt proposal to use the Land and Water Conservation Fund for new parkland purchases on existing parks. The Republican-controlled Senate Environment and Public Works Committee ignored Reagan's campaign pledges to the contrary and early signaled its intentions to block major changes in the Clean Air Act. Amid acrimonious exchanges with Environmental Protection Agency Administrator Anne Gorsuch and pleas by the panel for direction from the White House, nothing happened regarding the act in 1981. The Clean Air Act will be an issue again in 1982, as will other environmental matters. Heated confrontations between the White House and Congress are certain, and the president will probably not get his own way.

Foreign policy also provided another issue for wrangling by both ends of Pennsylvania Avenue in 1981. From the beginning it was clear that foreign policy would be more divisive in the Ninety-seventh Congress than economic policy. In the House of Representatives, whereas Democrats had been disorganized over the Reagan economic initiative, several early actions indicated a much more determined and directed opposition to a Reaganesque foreign policy. In December 1980 House Democrats on the Foreign Affairs Committee ousted one of their subcommittee chairmen and bypassed another contender to choose aggressive young liberals for the Latin America and Africa panels—choices made explicitly to form a counterweight to Ronald Reagan and Jesse Helms. In an even more provocative step, the same legislators took the innocuously titled subcommittee on "International Organizations" and renamed it "Human Rights and International Organizations." It would be hard to construct a clearer signal of policy differences.

On the Senate side, the president also had foreign policy problems, especially from his fellow Republicans, often on the right. For months Jesse Helms single-handedly blocked a string of Reagan nominees to high State Department positions, saying that they were insufficiently loyal to Reagan's goals. By an embarrassingly wide margin, the more centrist Foreign Relations Committee rejected the president's nominee for assistant secretary of state for human rights.

Both houses of Congress balked at Reagan's request for foreign aid, limiting aid and adding conditions to aid to El Salvador and Pakistan, among other places. Congress also spurned a presidential request to repeal the Clark amendment barring U.S. intervention in Angola. Both houses promptly passed, by overwhelming margins, resolutions condemning the U.S. vote in Geneva on international infant formula standards.

Foreign policy in Congress was by no means a total loss for the president. With his leadership, Congress passed the first foreign aid bill in three years; thanks to Reagan, twice as many Republicans as usual supported foreign aid. The president was able to push his various arms packages through Congress, albeit with strings and conditions attached. In the major showdown vote—sales of Airborne Warning and Control Systems (AWACS) planes to Saudi Arabia—the president won a dramatic 52-to-48 victory in the Senate, after conceding in the House (which thumbed its nose at the president by a 3-to-1 margin).

As I. M. Destler documents, there was little for the president to be elated about after the AWACS vote. According to most participants on both sides, it was an issue that never should have arisen. It was handled ineptly for months by overconfident and shortsighted presidential aides and was finally won by the president only after he had inflated it to dramatic proportions and paid a high political price to win the final votes. AWACS was less a victory than the avoidance of a defeat. The opposition to the president in the Republican Senate—led as it was by key Republicans—suggests more tough battles on foreign policy issues in Congress in the future. A president is usually given one major early victory by Congress to signal American unity to the world. This unity disappears soon afterward. Carter's early victory was the Panama Canal Treaty; Reagan's was the sale of AWACS.

A related subject is defense policy, on which the president encountered warning signals, not direct setbacks. The early, broad consensus on the need for increases in defense spending was strained during the budget process and broke down further over the specifics of weapons procurement. Still, there were no significant breaches in the president's defense guidelines.

A budget proposal that called for generous hikes in defense and dramatic cuts in social programs was almost inevitably going to face pressure to make cuts in defense expenditures. The pressure increased after August, when revised economic projections forecast a larger deficit and the president called for a second round of 1982 spending cuts. In a highly public internal battle, Budget Director David Stockman lost to Defense Secretary Caspar Weinberger in his effort to cut defense increases substantially. The president also rejected pleas from moderate Republican "gypsy moth" congressmen and from Senate chieftains Baker and Domenici to balance cuts in social programs with more cuts in defense. It will, however, be considerably more difficult to resist those demands when further social cuts are proposed for 1983.

The president also had problems with the substance of his defense plan. Months of embarrassing public scrutiny over the fate of the B-1 bomber and the basing mode for the MX missile ended in early

October with an announcement by Secretary Weinberger that satisfied no one. The strongest immediate criticism, ironically, came from Republican Senator John Tower, chairman of the Armed Services Committee, who accused Reagan of just about the worst sin he could imagine—creating a national defense weaker than Jimmy Carter's. The criticism was echoed by hawks and doves in both parties.

Nevertheless, Congress accepted for fiscal 1982 Reagan's B-1 and MX proposals. Part of the reason was Reagan's masterful "zero-option" arms reduction speech in November. Also important was the Republican unity and organization in the Senate. In December the Senate Democrats, led by Carl Levin and Gary Hart, used a brilliant strategy to contest the defense bill. Rather than challenge the Reagan proposals directly by calling for budget cuts (and thus leave themselves vulnerable to accusations of being weak on defense), the Democrats offered a string of amendments to add funds for politically popular and sound defense items, intending later to balance the additions with proposed cuts in the B-1 and MX. The strategy was clear to Republicans, and they united to block the seductively attractive Democratic amendments. In past years the Republican minority has used a similar strategy successfully, thanks to Democratic indiscipline. So far, at least, the Republican majority has proved stronger and far more disciplined than its predecessor.

The year 1982, however, might be different for defense. The rationale for supporting the president after his arms reduction speech —so that he could use the weapons as "bargaining chips"—will fade unless serious arms control talks begin. Budget-cutting pressure in the defense area will be even greater. Competition among defense programs for dollars—the 600-ship navy versus the B-1 bomber versus the Stealth bomber, and so on—will be heightened. Defense authorization and appropriations bills for fiscal 1983 are not likely to fare as well as did those for fiscal 1982.

In summary, then, the president won on some issues, lost on some, and compromised substantially on others. Without the budget and tax cuts, Reagan's first year was rather typical for a president, though still somewhat better than average. If the budget and tax cuts are factored in, however, it was, quite clearly, an extraordinary year.

The Prospects for 1982

Will 1982 also be an extraordinary year for President Reagan? There are a number of reasons—including the president's budget and tax successes—to believe that it will not. Rather, 1982 is likely to be a year of protracted conflict and stalemate between the president and Congress, with few striking policy advances.

One reason is the budget and tax cuts themselves. We have amply described the substantial dividends they paid to the president; we have not yet assessed their costs. Many of the bills he must pay have not yet come due. One important cost to the president is in his limited *future ability to shape flexible coalitions.* Three times the president bucked the odds and formed a winning coalition in the House on budgets and taxes. Three times he spurned appeals for compromise by House Democratic leaders, and forged a majority composed of unified Republicans and a splinter group of Democrats. Three times he publicly and triumphantly humiliated the Democrats and their leaders. The first time was necessary and important. The second and third occasions were less so. Understandably, the Democrats wanted retribution and revenge—desires well expressed by Jim Wright in his "diary" in the *Washington Post* in December.[2] Democrats who honestly believe that they made a good-faith effort to meet the president on the reconciliation package and on the tax cuts, and who were coldly spurned in the process, are much less likely to respond to the president when he needs them in the future. He will need their support on social security, foreign aid, social issues, block grants, and many other questions on which Republicans will not be so united.

The end-of-session experience in December gives some indication that the cost may not be overly burdensome to the president. He won the vote on a farm bill because of the key support of House Democratic Whip Tom Foley. Foley supported the bill not to return any favors to the White House, but because of his pragmatic calculation that it was in the best interest of farmers. The president succeeded in getting foreign aid authorization and appropriations bills because he had the support of many more Republicans than usually vote for foreign aid. If he can continue to frame issues so that Democrats feel compelled to support him, and if he can continue to maintain unusually high Republican cohesion, the president will not need to court Democratic leaders. Yet the margins of victory on the farm and foreign aid votes were very slim. A decision last August to increase the level of public humiliation for O'Neill, Wright, Foley, and others may not appear so wise by next August. In any event, it would be a painless and sensible move for Reagan to make some direct bridge-building efforts now to Wright, Foley, Gillis Long, Jim Jones, and Dan Rostenkowski.

The budget program will have other costs in 1982. By forcing early omnibus votes on the budget resolution and reconciliation, the president both compressed and reversed normal congressional sched-

2. David S. Broder, "Diary of a Mad Majority Leader," *The Washington Post Outlook,* December 13, 1981.

ules, requiring other parts of the process to be delayed and extended. To win the early votes, the White House used a set of highly exaggerated assumptions, a fact known to virtually everyone even as the program was debated. The collapse of these assumptions caused the president to send to Congress a second set of budget cuts for 1982, confusing congressional decision making over appropriations and budget resolutions even further, and generating the December confrontation over the continuing resolution. With presidential economic assumptions now shattered, and in the aftermath of the continuing resolution, the budget process in 1982 will be a long, drawn-out affair.

Thus, in part because of the novel approach the president took to the budget in his first year, budget and tax questions will continue to dominate through 1982. Much of the 1982 budget, including numerous appropriations bills, was left unfinished and unsigned when Congress recessed for the holidays. When Congress returns at the end of January, it faces work not only on the remaining 1982 appropriations (including any that President Reagan decides to veto) but also on another 1982 continuing resolution that must pass by March, some possible supplemental spending bills to tie up loose ends left by the existing continuing resolution, and a possible third budget resolution. At the same time, Congress must gear up to consider the overall 1983 budget, which includes its own impressive array of controversial cuts.

The budget crunch comes at a time when Congress is more concerned about individual proposed cutbacks, less convinced by Reagan's economic assumptions and advisers, and less in awe of the president's political mystique. For his own part, the president, stubbornly resisting pressure from his Republican lieutenants in Congress to scale down his budget cuts, make more cuts in defense and entitlement programs, and increase revenues, is likely to veto a few appropriations bills to show his determination and consistency—thus requiring even more congressional attention to money matters.

This scenario clearly, then, will *not* fit the earlier White House plan to concentrate on the president's economic package in the first half of 1981, so these issues could later be "put aside" to tackle social and foreign policy questions. If anything—given the coming budget crunch outlined above—we will see even *more* preoccupation than before with battles over basic budget priorities.

The controversy and conflict over the administration's policy toward deficits, tax expenditures, "revenue enhancement," defense, entitlement programs, and the "safety net" will compound the 1983 budget battles. Reagan was able to force the timing on reconciliation in 1981 because he faced a Democratic leadership that had been battered in the 1980 election. He had a unified and coherent set of policies and a credible group of advisers (led by Budget Director David Stockman). There was strong public sentiment that the new president at least deserved a chance. The Democrats are no longer *as* dizzy and demoralized as they were a year ago. The president's own advisers disagree on the basic elements of his program. Stockman's personal credibility is badly eroded, and the president is no longer a "new" president.

Taken together, these factors promise a long, tough, drawn-out battle. The battle lines will be drawn more closely by a Democratic party that has felt both feisty and energized since September. As we noted earlier, the House Democratic leadership saw its humiliation increase geometrically with each successive early Reagan victory; revenge has been on their minds ever since. With the Republican disarray over deficits, tax increases, and interest rates, the Democrats were given a tangible reason for optimism. The sense of uncertainty in Republican ranks over basic policy has made the once uncertain Democrats more confident that they can openly oppose the president and, over time, quite possibly win their share of the battles.

The administration and Republican leaders in Congress recognize these problems and will adjust their strategies accordingly. Given their likely response, we can expect *an attempt to change budget priorities without a budget, by means of the continued creative use of reconciliation and continuing resolutions.* The president will probably veto any 1982 appropriations bills that exceed the spending levels set in the stopgap continuing spending resolution that expires in March. Rather than focus efforts heavily on passing a full budget with all the trimmings for 1983, he will wait for another omnibus continuing resolution.

Thus the president will try to combine a small number of highly publicized showdown votes with broader, behind-the-scenes trench warfare, including rescissions, deferrals, and vetoes involving individual appropriations bills and items in continuing resolutions. The president has some big advantages and will make some progress. Because he will have less control over the timing of votes than he possessed in 1981, and less ability to hold his coalition together, the most likely outcome is *protracted conflict and stalemate, which will accelerate as we approach November.* The chance of getting a fiscal 1983 budget into law before the end of 1983 is very, very slim.

The likelihood that President Reagan will win on these and other issues in 1982 will be lessened for another, obvious reason: *1982 is an election year.* Every member of the House and one-third of the Senate are up for election in November. The first result is that legislative calculations change and tend to be compressed into a shorter-term focus. As one vulnerable "gypsy moth" moderate Republican put it recently, "My neck's on the chopping block—not Reagan's. He can talk about longer-term solutions to interest rates and unemployment. I can't. I need something to tell my people now." As each day passes, we move further away from the flush of Republican victory in November 1980 to the difficulty of running as the in-party in November 1982. Members of Congress who earlier gratefully basked in the limelight of Reagan's success begin to maneuver for some campaign insurance against the possibility of Reagan's failure. If the recession continues well into 1982, with unemployment on the rise and few visible signs of incipient recovery, the nervousness among Republican incumbents and candidates will increase. Having a few visible votes against the president's programs enables a legislator to advertise his independence, to say if necessary, "Don't blame me—blame him." Thus, we can expect the incredible Republican party unity, which approached 100 percent on key 1981 votes, to decline somewhat in 1982. If that level of support falls to the still respectable 85 to 90 percent range, the president will be in trouble.

Although an election year is always different from a nonelection year, 1982 has other features that will alter presidential relations and policy from 1981. It is a reapportionment and redistricting election year. Much press and public attention has been focused on which party will gain most from reapportionment. More important for policy and the president, though, is the simple fact of redistricting. Whether a state gains or loses seats, or an individual legislator sees his base disappear, there is a broader process at work: *Virtually all the members of the House of Representatives will see their districts change significantly for 1982.* Under the principle of "one man–one vote," all districts must be equal in population, with figures based on the 1980 census. As a result, all districts (except in states such as Wyoming and Alaska, which have only one House seat) have been realigned; old constituents, familiar with the incumbent's name and record, are shuffled to other seats; new constituents, who don't know the incumbent from Adam (or from the challenger) are added.

Redistricting means uncertainty for congressmen. It compels them to go back home more frequently to protect their political base and develop a rapport with new voters. It also means more opportunities for challengers, and thus an even greater incentive for incumbent legislators to campaign.

Every election year brings pressure to shorten congressional workweeks, provide longer weekends for campaigning, and end the legislative session no later than August. This pressure is increased in a redistricting election year. The unprecedented partisanship and the bitterness of the 1982 redistricting effort will increase the pressure to compress the 1982 congressional session.

The implications of an abbreviated legislative year in 1982 are manifold. A large number of substantive legislative proposals were postponed in 1981 for the total effort required for the Reagan economic package. The list of policy items waiting for consideration in 1982 is thus already long—but the time available for their consideration will be much shorter.

Because budget and tax questions will require so much work, as we have already discussed, Congress probably will not be willing or able to do much else. Congressional workweeks will be short, and adjournment will come early—thus the agenda will be severely curtailed. If Congress concentrates on the FY 1982 and 1983 budgets, deals with any surprises, emergencies, or exigencies like filibusters, then there will not be much time left for congressional action on social security, the Clean Air Act, criminal justice, the criminal code, Voting Rights Act extension, banking regulation, defense policy (such as MX basing and the 600-ship Navy), the Davis-Bacon Act, tuition tax credits, Namibia, aid to El Salvador, bilateral and multilateral foreign aid policy, natural gas deregulation, and block grant expansion or changes in Medicaid. Then, of course, there are the social issues of busing, abortion, and school prayer, which have been less than patiently awaiting their promised turn in 1982.

Some of these substantive issues were slated to be considered in 1981, but for various reasons were delayed or postponed. Both the House Energy and Commerce Committee and the Senate Environment and Public Works panel, for example, were geared up early last year to consider and pass a revision of the Clean Air Act. As we noted earlier, however, repeated mixed, conflicting, or absent signals from the administration on its desires and specific proposals led to postponement and limited congressional action. Little if any far-reaching change can be expected from either committee, even if the White House were to adopt an alternative and support it vigorously. In any event, few participants will have the stomach for a protracted fight in 1982 to dilute this major environmental law. Any significant change in the clean air standards would be controversial, demanding substantial time for debate. Senate Majority Leader Howard Baker will be less than excited at the prospect of devoting several weeks of a rapidly shrinking Senate calendar to a tough squabble over air pollution.

Some of the pending substantive issues may be handled in a backdoor fashion through reconciliation, but in general most difficult policy questions will be postponed until 1983. We can, however, expect tough and bitter voting on knotty social issues, pushed by "New Right" conservatives like Helms and East, and filibustered in the Senate by liberals like Weicker and Metzenbaum (or vice versa, in the case of the Voting

Rights Act). There is one caveat here. Although most of the substantive issues will see much motion but little movement in 1982, the final days of the 1982 session will doubtless end in the unpredictable passage of a number of surprise measures. In the past several years, Congress's desire to recess at the end of a session has clashed strongly with the pent-up demand to finish action on the stockpile of unpassed bills. In the last-minute zoo-like flurry of late-night sessions, some bills are passed that should never be passed and other measures die an undeserved death. In 1982, the desire of Congress to recess in August and to hit the campaign trail will be stronger than usual; so too will the pressure from the backlog of unpassed bills on important issues. Thus the final days of the Ninety-seventh Congress will be very interesting ones to watch—and no one can predict their product.

What about the tax increases and entitlement reductions proposed by, among others, Senate Budget Committee Chairman Pete V. Domenici? The budget battles will undoubtedly increase the pressure to find new sources of revenue and to cut social security benefits. Yet, *more than half* of the members of the Senate Finance Committee, including six of the eleven Republicans, are up for reelection in 1982. The committee handles all tax matters, as well as trade and social security. Many of the panel's members, including Chafee, Wallop, Durenberger, Bentsen, and Mitchell, face potentially difficult election contests. They will scarcely want to vote for election-year cuts in social security benefits or to spend extra hours in Washington debating excise tax increases or value-added taxes—unless the president forces them to do so by reversing himself and pushing strongly for "revenue enhancement." The controversial issue of leasing, however, along with closing various "loopholes" and imposing a windfall profits tax on natural gas, are politically more palatable and attractive issues for the committee to consider without any presidential nudging. They are likely to receive hearings, at least. In the case of leasing, we can expect even more than hearings from the House Ways and Means Committee. Should the economy continue to falter, the Republican-controlled finance panel might well also entertain a variety of trade protection measures, probably beginning with steel.

All these factors together have other political consequences. We can expect signs of tension to develop between the president and Republican leaders on the one hand, and conservatives on the other. With the president's desire to keep Congress's attention and efforts focused on the budget and the economy, filibusters over busing or flaps over abortion-related amendments to appropriations bills will not be well received, either in the White House or in the offices of Republican leaders Howard Baker and Robert Michel. Baker in particular will have his hands full, given the Senate's notorious inability to keep on schedule. If there is an additional loud clamor from staunch conservatives such as Symms and Grassley to guarantee a balanced budget in 1984, even if their solution means upsetting delicate budget negotiations between the White House, Republican leaders, and moderates in both parties, relations between the president and Congress could worsen.

Conclusion

The year 1981 was a striking and unusual year in the interaction between the president and Congress. The year 1982, however, will seem more like business as usual. Instead of bold movement in broad-brush strokes by an assertive, persuasive, and popular president, we are likely to find more modest, piecemeal change, accompanied by protracted conflict each step along the way. Change will occur, and it will be in Reagan's direction, but it will be more incremental and more drawn out. Few pieces of nonbudget legislation will make it through the presidential/congressional labyrinth. We can expect fewer signs of a "Reagan Revolution," and more of the guerrilla warfare that typifies American politics and policy making.

For other presidents in other times, this scenario has been a common pattern. Paul Light has demonstrated convincingly that a president's first year is crucial.[3] If any presidential domestic agenda is set, it is done in the first year; each succeeding year becomes more difficult, as presidential popularity wanes and congressional intractability increases. Even our most successful modern presidents—Wilson, the two Roosevelts, Johnson—accomplished more in their first year of the presidency than later. The least successful presidents, in contrast, did not take advantage of opportunities presented to them in their initial years, and went downhill from a much lower altitude.

First-year success for a president does not necessarily mean that history will acclaim him. How he handles the remaining years of the presidency is also significant. Lyndon Johnson is judged as much by the failures of 1967–1968 as by the victories of 1964–1965. Although Ronald Reagan's smashing success in setting an agenda in 1981 has helped enormously in establishing a policy foundation and forging a positive presidential reputation, he still needs an economic upturn and legislative successes in 1982 and beyond if he is to continue to receive a favorable judgment on his presidency.

3. Paul C. Light, "The President's Agenda: Notes on the Timing of Domestic Choice," *Presidential Studies Quarterly*, vol. 11, no. 1 (Winter 1981), pp. 67-82.

Even though 1982 will present formidable challenges for the president's program, this does not necessarily suggest an inevitable or drastic decline in the stature and reputation of Ronald Reagan. Reagan has proved himself a tough and adaptable competitor in the Washington policy arena. His years as governor of California showed him to be a pragmatic realist in action, if a fiery ideologue in rhetoric. The "all or nothing" approach that worked for Reagan on the budget and tax votes in 1981 may not work again in 1982. But if Reagan maintains his personal popularity, a clever legislative strategy of public feistiness and backroom compromise could sustain his strong reputation as a leader. Even so, the reality will be much less real change in policy than 1981 provided or 1982 earlier promised.